What started out as an endo<del>rsement</del> ... ally declaring the prayers outlined in this book. This is a must-read for all deliverance workers in the trenches needing self-deliverance!

—Apostle Alexander Pagani
Pastor, Amazing Church; Author, *The Secrets to Deliverance* and *The Secrets to Generational Curses*

I am thrilled to see John Ramirez continue to tackle the topic of spiritual warfare in *Fire Prayers*. This book is a powerful tool for those who want to destroy the works of Satan and be effective in spiritual warfare. There is a great deal of value in the topics covered in this book, including the prayers of renunciation, repentance, and spiritual covering over your home and family, and especially the specific prayers against certain demons that may be trying to destroy your life. Whether you are young in your understanding or seasoned in spiritual warfare, this book can greatly benefit you and your faith. I pray God inspires you through *Fire Prayers* to wage war against the kingdom of darkness and claim His victory in your life.

—Vladimir Savchuk
Pastor, Hungry Generation Church;
Author, *Break Free*

I can't recommend this book enough! *Fire Prayers* provides a comprehensive guide to understanding the spiritual battles we face every day and equips readers with powerful prayers and strategies for overcoming them. John Ramirez makes the complex topic of spiritual warfare accessible to new believers and mature believers alike. The book is filled with scriptural references and real-life examples, making it both informative and practical. Overall, this is an invaluable resource for anyone seeking to get off the sidelines and get on the frontlines.

—Isaiah Saldivar
Revivalist; Deliverance Minister

In *Fire Prayers*, John Ramirez does a great job illustrating how to walk in your God-given destiny by showing us how to effectively wage war against Satan and the forces of darkness. Throughout the book you can feel the heartbeat of the Father calling His children to rise and walk in victory!

—Daniel Adams
Founder, The Supernatural Life;
Author, *Supernatural Living*

JOHN RAMIREZ

FIRE PRAYERS

CHARISMA HOUSE

Text in braces {} in the AMP OR AMPC was added by the author.

Visit the author's website at https://johnramirez.org.

Cataloging-in-Publication Data is on file with the Library of Congress.
International Standard Book Number: 978-1-63641-155-2
E-book ISBN: 978-1-63641-156-9

While the author has made every effort to provide accurate internet addresses at the time of publication, neither the publisher nor the author assumes any responsibility for errors or for changes that occur after publication. Further, the publisher does not have any control over and does not assume any responsibility for author or third-party websites or their content.

23 24 25 26 27 — 9 8 7 6 5 4 3 2
Printed in the United States of America

CONTENTS

Part III: Covering Your Home, Family, Well-Being, Destiny, and Church

ACKNOWLEDGMENTS

I DEDICATE THIS BOOK to King Jesus, and I thank Him for this incredible opportunity as a kingdom secretary writing to equip the saints to fight the good fight. I thank God that He loves the misfit. That is my story. Holy Spirit, thank You so much for giving me the revelation and clarity to write this incredible book.

Catherine: I am incredibly blessed and honored to have met you, the love of my life. You are a gift from God, and I love you unconditionally. You are a phenomenal woman of God and an amazing wife. You are a tremendous minister with a powerful testimony. Words cannot describe how much I love you and am in love with you. I am beyond grateful to the Lord Jesus Christ for all we will do together and for the great and awesome memories we are making on the journey the Lord has given us.

Mom: You are one of my heroes. You have been widowed twice and had major surgeries. You have lost a son and a daughter. Your trust and love are in King Jesus Christ. You are an example of valor in Christ, always putting Him first. You came out of a demonic religion and then had a hospital encounter with Jesus Christ. You almost died five times in one day, but the Lord sent a bunch of Christians to lead you to the cross of Jesus Christ. Your life has never been the same. I thank Jesus for giving me such a precious mother.

Amanda: I am so proud of you. You have endured many storms, some of them even now. But God is writing your story. I have had dreams about you being on bigger platforms than your daddy. You are going to make Jesus Christ proud because He has a purpose and destiny for you. Whatever I don't finish on the earth God will continue through you. I'm proud of you and proud to be your dad. I love you unconditionally and will never stop loving you. I will always be here for you.

Andrew: I am so glad I'm your Papa John. I see Jesus' hand on your life and am so proud to call you my stepson. God is going to do beautiful things in your life that will outshine your expectations. You are an incredible young man, and you will be an awesome man of God. I consider myself your spiritual dad, and I am always here for you—any time, any day. I'm in your corner, cheering you on.

Inner circle: My church, my spiritual gangsters, my OG—you are one of a kind. You are all deeply special to me, wherever you live, in the States or around the globe. You are my spiritual family, my special ops, and my spiritual snipers—the "unknowns" God is going to use to usher in the end-time kingdom of Jesus Christ. You are an outstanding community of believers: untouchable, unmovable, and unshakable. I see the fire of the Holy Spirit in your eyes.

Raoul: You are an amazing man of God. I thank Him for you every day. You are a true friend. I am so blessed that you were home that day and turned on the television. I am thankful for what you heard and for your reaching out to me. I will never forget that testimony. We are on this amazing journey together.

Leticia: You are an incredible woman of God and have been a blessing in my life. I am grateful that you teamed up with Raoul so we can touch the world for Jesus Christ through my books, especially this one.

Charisma Media: Thank you for the opportunity to turn a new page and be part of your publishing family. Together we are going to touch the world for Jesus Christ. This book makes it a bad season for the devil. We're going to arm the saints around the world. Thank you, Charisma Media, for this great and awesome opportunity.

Cheri Swalwell: I thank God for you, my sister. I am so blessed and honored to have you (the author of *Sisters in Christ: Defeat the Enemy One Powerful Prayer at a Time*) on my side, doing the unbelievable task of typing my book. I admire you deeply as a vessel of honor who is touching women worldwide with your ministry and with the love of Jesus Christ.

Phil Lee, PhD, and In-Young Choi, PhD: I am beyond grateful to have both of you in my life. You are handpicked by God and have deeply blessed and touched my life, loving and caring for me unconditionally. I feel the same way about you. We are a team, winning souls together. You are two of the most creative minds I have ever seen. I rejoice that you are my brother and sister in Christ. Thank you so much for being in my life.

Pastors and leaders: Thank you for allowing me to preach in your churches and share the battlefield in setting the captives free. You are so courageous and bold in Christ. So many pastors love talking about the devil without confronting him. I thank God for people like you. I salute you in Jesus Christ, and I thank you from the bottom of my heart. You make Him proud.

My brothers and sisters: Thank you, whether believers or non-believers, for trusting John Ramirez Ministries to touch your lives through the e-courses and books the Holy Spirit has given me. To all the saints around the world who are being equipped by these materials to be armed and dangerous ambassadors and arrows in God's quiver: we are team Jesus. Thank you all.

My dear friends; my sister in the Lord, Bethel; my sister Jody; and my incredible sister Jessica: From the bottom of my heart, I thank you for standing with this ministry financially, through prayer, and in trust. You have given unconditionally, with all generosity.

The people sending support through Tithe.ly and PayPal: I salute you from the depths of my heart for giving from your financial resources to support this ministry in reaching the world for Jesus Christ. Thank you so much. I'm deeply touched and grateful for each one of you.

ENGAGE OR SUFFER LOSS

Don't misjudge or be ignorant about the enemy of your soul. If you lack knowledge about him, you will find yourself sitting in defeat where bondage and misery rule and reign.

Ask me how I know.

I remember being a little boy in the South Bronx, standing in a lot scattered with broken glass and other debris. I called that lot a playground. Little did I know that as my friend and I hung out there, a necklace would fall from the second heaven, carrying the seven demonic powers of the dark side. Grabbing that demonic key would eventually usher me into the highest levels of the satanic kingdom's hierarchy.

It was bad enough that I came from a bloodline of warlocks and witches on my father's side of the family. Now my innocence was robbed. I entered the portals of the demonic, where I spent the next twenty-five years of my life. I eventually sat with the devil himself, astral-projecting to countries and regions and altering atmospheres in the spirit realm. One October 31, I got married in a demonic Halloween wedding. I was baptized at the highest level of witches, warlocks, and demons.

That all changed when Jesus saved me. He took the pen out of my hand and wrote my story His way. The witches, warlocks, and devil worshippers still come after me, but I have bad news for them: I bear the mark of Jesus Christ. By His grace, I will finish my race and make my King proud that He picked me.

That is the point of this book. You might be surrounded by darkness and defeat. Even if you are not openly associating with the devil, you feel him breathing down your neck. I know the feeling. But I also know that the rest of your story is yet to be written. Your race can have a beautiful ending, and Jesus will be proud that He chose you. But you will have to engage. Those who don't engage suffer loss.

Keep reading. I wrote this book for you.

KNOW YOUR ENEMY; KNOW HIS DEMONIC STRATEGIES

A lot of churches dislike saying this, but Satan is a master con artist, deceiver, and general on the battlefield. Just look at his résumé: he has been fighting since the day he was cast out of heaven. That is when King Jesus hit him so hard that he forgot his name.

Satan is effective in his wiles and schemes. His kingdom is very well established. His monitoring spirits, spirits of entrapment, and spirits of hindrance and delay are tormenting and afflicting believers in the worldwide church of Jesus Christ. Satan loves to explore our weaknesses using his setups and the open doors of generational curses. He uses whatever he can use against us. So let's stop taking him lightly. Let's quit talking about him and start confronting him once and for all.

Start by understanding the enemy of your soul. Learn to recognize his setups. He uses many weapons and methods of attack in the realm of the spirit, including these:

- dreams of false practices and false realities (Some dreams that pose as truth are from the enemy.)

- strange fire, mixture of the holy with the profane

- mystical belief systems that seem credible but are not

- occult practices

- mind control

- oppression on every level (spirit, soul, body, family, finances, relationships, and so on)

- satanic doors (means of entry):
  - eye gates and ear gates that are open to filth, music, gossip, lies, and so on through what we watch and listen to. Proverbs 4:20–22 warns us to protect our eye and ear gates: "My son, pay attention to my words and be willing to learn; *open your ears to my sayings.*

> *Do not let them escape from your sight*; keep them in
> the center of your heart. For they are life to those who
> find them, and healing and health to all their flesh"
> (emphasis added).

◈ mouth gates that are open through what we speak.
Proverbs 18:21 says, "Death and life are in the power of
the tongue, and those who love it and indulge it will eat
its fruit and bear the consequences of their words."

- other satanic fiery darts involving rejection, unforgiveness,
fear, anxiety, sorrow, emptiness, misery, and confusion

That's just part of the devil's playbook. I can tell you from my long
experience in his camp that he wants believers to sleep but not rest. This
kind of restlessness is an open door. The devil wants believers to entertain demonic dreams all night and all day. He wants them to doubt God's
character and live prayerless lives. He wants them to be occupied with
insignificant things that steal their time with God.

The million-dollar question is, *Why are we misjudging the enemy of
our souls?* The Bible shows that Jesus Christ took the devil seriously in
every encounter. It's time for us to rise up from our spiritual denial and
slumber, put on Christ, confront the enemy, and be set free.

Start at the Beginning

Notice that I mention *believers.* I am speaking now to all my precious
brothers and sisters, whom I love with all my heart: before you pray the
prayers in this book, you must first be in right standing with Jesus Christ.
In other words, you must be a born-again believer, sanctified and washed
in His blood. Through your faith you become secure in Christ Jesus as
your Lord and Savior, believing that

- He is the Son of God who came to die on the cross for the
sins of the world (your sins and mine),

- He was resurrected on the third day and sits at the right
hand of the Father (Heb. 1:3), and

- He is coming back to establish His kingdom on the earth forever.

Before you begin praying the awesome prayers in this book to destroy the works of darkness and live the life Jesus Christ offers, say this short prayer aloud:

Father God, I come in the name of Your holy Son, Jesus. I confess the sins of my heart, my mouth, and my thinking and ask for forgiveness for all my trespasses and iniquities. Please forgive me. Jesus, come into my heart. Be my Lord and Savior. I put my trust and faith in the finished work of Your cross. I ask You, Holy Spirit, to come into my heart today. I give You back the pen and ask You to write my story. As I go through the pages of this book, reveal by Your power every area of my life that needs to be made right. I renounce whatever is not of You, including any generational issues or doors that I have opened, any ungodliness that is in my own life, and any family curses that are affecting me. Please help me realize what I must put on Your fire altar. In the mighty, untouchable, unmovable name of Jesus Christ, my Lord and Savior, amen.

Cover Yourself With the Blood of Jesus Christ

Now let me complete my thought: *cover yourself with the blood of Jesus Christ from the crown of your head to the soles of your feet, hold the promises of the Lord up high, and walk in the principles of His kingdom.* Knowing your enemy is important. Knowing the truth about Jesus is even more important. Before you pray the fire prayers that close the chapter, declare these scriptures and make them your prayers too:

If you acknowledge and confess with your mouth that Jesus is Lord [recognizing His power, authority, and majesty as God], and believe in your heart that God raised Him from the dead, you will be saved.

—Romans 10:9

They overcame and conquered him because of the blood of the Lamb and because of the word of their testimony, for they did not love their life and renounce their faith even when faced with death.

—Revelation 12:11

Fire Prayers

By the words I speak through faith in Christ Jesus, I stand in the power of the Holy Spirit, I believe God's Word, and I trust the Holy Spirit who lives in me. In Jesus' name, amen.

I believe and trust that Jesus is the only way to God, heaven, and eternal life. I believe that Jesus Christ is my Lord and Savior. I have no other gods and no idols in my heart. Jesus Christ is my one and only. I put my faith and trust in the Father, the Son, and the Holy Spirit. In Jesus' name, amen.

It is written in my heart that Jesus Christ's precious blood and the finished work of the cross wiped me clean from the crown of my head to the soles of my feet (1 John 1:9; 2:1–2). He is in me, and I am in Him (John 17:21; 2 Cor. 5:17). I have eternal life with Jesus, my King.

By the Holy Spirit's power working in me, I believe that strength and might come with the anointing God has given me through the blood of Jesus Christ. I declare and decree that I will be set free, completely and fully. In the unmatched name of Jesus Christ, amen.

As I pray, I declare and decree that I cover myself and my mind, heart, and soul; my house, child(ren), family, and loved ones; and my ministry, church, purpose, and destiny with the blood of Jesus Christ. His blood is the shield over me and over everything I declare—not only for my good but also for every-thing He has placed in my heart. Let every attack of the devil and his demons, every satanic altar that bears my name, and every plot and scheme the devil has set for me be destroyed, completely and fully, by the power of Jesus' name. Amen.

Holy Spirit, as I pray these prayers, I ask You to make me invisible to all satanic forces and any demonic monitoring system that tries to come against me and my freedom. In Jesus' name, amen.

By the anointing and power of the Lord Jesus Christ, I break off from me every hindrance, delay, blockage, and distraction that would stop me from receiving answers to this book's prayers for my life, ministry, purpose, destiny, family, marriage, child(ren), career, job, and everything God has entrusted to me, including my salvation and my relationship with the Lord Jesus Christ. In Jesus' name, amen.

PART I

LAYING THE GROUNDWORK

Chapter 1
THE MINISTRY OF VIOLENCE

JESUS SAID THAT "from the days of John the Baptist until now the kingdom of heaven suffers violent assault, and violent men seize it by force [as a precious prize]" (Matt. 11:12). The apostle Paul was no stranger to this ministry of violence. He told us how to prepare, and he also told us how to engage:

> Be strong in the Lord [draw your strength from Him and be empowered through your union with Him] and in the power of His [boundless] might. Put on the full armor of God [for His precepts are like the splendid armor of a heavily-armed soldier], so that you may be able to [successfully] stand up against all the schemes and the strategies and the deceits of the devil. For our struggle is not against flesh and blood [contending only with physical opponents], but against the rulers, against the powers, against the world forces of this [present] darkness, against the spiritual forces of wickedness in the heavenly (supernatural) places.
>
> —EPHESIANS 6:10–12

We see the pain and the misery around the world and what the demonic kingdom has done to humankind. We first fell into sin in the Garden of Eden, and the violence began. In history's first murder, Cain shed his brother Abel's blood. Violence continued throughout the Bible's pages, and it continues in the world today. We hear the cries of children aborted in their mothers' wombs. We hear the myths about abortion being good for us. Around the world, there are stories of premature death, infirmity, and demonic oppression and possession that attack precious believers. Division and discord persist among the races, and the sin of oppression continues. We have witnessed murders wreaking havoc in our schools, shootings devastating our churches, and fake news teaming up with the devil himself. Families are breaking down and divorce rates are rising in our churches. There is debauchery in the house of God, even

3

though Jesus warned two thousand years ago, "'My house shall be called a house of prayer'; but you are making it a robbers' den" (Matt. 21:13).

The devil and his cronies are having a field day. But there is good news! The devil is defeated by the finished work of the cross. Satan's time is short. Exodus 15:3 reminds us that "the LORD is a warrior; the LORD is His name."

It's time to fight back. We are on the victor's side.

DISCERN THE SPIRITUAL CONFLICT

What exactly is the ministry of violence? It is the spiritual conflict that no child of God can afford to sweep under the rug. Remember, those who don't engage suffer spiritual loss. You cannot ignore the ministry of violence and be more than a conqueror in Christ Jesus (Rom. 8:37).

If you want your God-given destiny to be fulfilled in the land of the living, you have to recognize how critical this ministry is. We are in the last hour, but examples from the Scriptures still guide us. Look at David's life: he was a man of war who killed the giant Goliath and fought many battles. We fight the same spiritual battles today, but do we recognize them? Hosea 4:6 tells us, "My people are destroyed for lack of knowledge [of My law, where I reveal My will]. Because you [the priestly nation] have rejected knowledge, I will also reject you from being My priest. Since you have forgotten the law of your God, I will also forget your children."

This is not the time to sleep. It's time to wake up, wear the armor of God, and put on Christ (Rom. 13:14). The battle is ongoing. You have been called by the Most High God and are enlisted in the almost untouchable, unmovable army of King Jesus. The battle is real, but if the devil couldn't kill you in your B.C. (before Christ) days, he is even less able to do it now.

God wants "to keep Satan from taking advantage of us; for we are not ignorant of his schemes" (2 Cor. 2:11). The apostle Paul said that "our struggle is not against flesh and blood [contending only with physical opponents], but against the rulers, against the powers, against the world forces of this [present] darkness, against the spiritual forces of wickedness in the heavenly (supernatural) places" (Eph. 6:12).

We don't aim our spiritual warfare at people; we fight the forces of wickedness in high places. Stop fighting the friend, child, spouse, or coworker who offended you. You're wasting time and falling into the enemy's entrapment. The battle is not about flesh and blood. It's about demonic spirits and wickedness in high places (Eph. 6:12). The one manipulating you to fight the wrong fight is a demon spirit. To be armed, dangerous, and supernaturally effective in waging war against the forces of hell, just do what Paul said: "Be strong in the Lord" (Eph. 6:10). It's about being spiritually mature. That comes through total submission to the Holy Spirit and the Word of God. It requires obedience to Christ, an attitude of humility, and standing in righteousness. Instead of acting on your emotions or carnal mindsets, maintain holiness and right standing in Christ. Let them show up in your lifestyle. Being strong in the Lord means surrendering yourself completely to Christ. Then you will access all He has prepared for you in the fight.

No devil can easily manipulate a person who is strong in the Spirit of Jesus Christ. Here's what the Lord says: "I...will be a wall of fire around {Jerusalem/God's people} [protecting her from enemies], and I will be the glory in her midst" (Zech. 2:5). The devil is no match for God.

Now let me share some spiritual warfare strategies that make us champions in the battle.

KNOW THE TRUTH THAT WILL SET YOU FREE

John 8:32 says, "You will know the truth [regarding salvation], and the truth will set you free [from the penalty of sin]." Study Scripture and memorize God's Word. Then, when the devil shows up, use it as the sword of the Spirit against the forces of darkness (Eph. 6:17). Let it form the prayers that come out of your mouth. That is what Jesus did in the wilderness when Satan came with three of the evilest temptations on the planet (Matt. 4:1–11). When the devil tried to entrap Jesus, He fought back by speaking God's Word. King Jesus defeated Satan right on the spot.

The number one weapon for believers is realizing that the more we live in God's Word, the more discernment, revelation, and clarity we have against the forces of darkness.

BE A SPIRITUAL SNIPER

Stop aiming the weapons in your arsenal and missing the target. Fire on the devil's setups, wiles, and schemes. Aim at any demonic altars or entrapments that have your name on them. Launch some fire prayers!

Here are some keys to praying effectively: Stop praying from your emotions. Pray from your spirit. Emotion-based prayers are powerless against satanic forces. Mix your prayers with faith, and target whatever is plaguing you (it has a name), tormenting you (it has an assignment), or afflicting you (be specific). Every infirmity in your body—whether cancer, diabetes, high blood pressure, heart attack, or multiple sclerosis—has a name. Each ailment is from the devil's arsenal, and each one has a target. But you have the faith, power, anointing, and fire of the Holy Spirit to make all of them shrivel up and die, in the name and blood of Jesus.

Break every demonic stronghold, and put the judgment of God on those demons. Don't let them escape from your prayer closet. Shut the door spiritually, and let them be tormented by the blood of Jesus, the Word of God, and the anointing you carry. Use the authority God has given you. Let those devils know that you've been with Jesus. Who are they compared with Jesus? That's how you fight. That's how you develop spiritual maturity.

King David was a man of war. He declared, "Arise, O LORD; save me, O my God! For You have struck all my enemies on the cheek; You have shattered the teeth of the wicked" (Ps. 3:7). That's a violent prayer! I'm not talking about punching people. I'm talking about breaking down, destroying, dismantling, and cursing to the root satanic forces, demonic forces, and the demonic assignments, strongholds, and bondages the devil wants to use to spiritually incarcerate you. Put the fire of the Holy Spirit on every demon's head and claim your victory. It's time to be more than a conqueror in Christ Jesus. Start and finish every assignment. God is a God of purpose and brings everything to completion.

ENGAGE THE ENEMY OF YOUR SOUL

Second Corinthians 10:4 says, "The weapons of our warfare are not physical [weapons of flesh and blood]. Our weapons are divinely powerful for the destruction of fortresses."

The devil wants to yank God's plan from your life, but as a believer you are heavily armed. "The thief comes only in order to steal and kill and destroy," but Jesus came so we "may have and enjoy life, and have it in abundance [to the full, till it overflows]" (John 10:10). You cannot negotiate with the enemy of your soul. Stop compromising and making peace with him. All he understands is violence. Satan draws you into his fight to destroy you because he *hates* you. Do you know why he hates you? First, you are made in the image of God. Second, you took over his job of worshipping Christ.

Fire prayers, whether in earthly languages or in the heavenly language of tongues (described in chapter 3), are the violent weapons God has given you to pull down strongholds and destroy the schemes Satan has set against you. Don't let fear rule you. It is not from God but is the devil's biggest weapon. It paralyzes you and brings torment. Look what happened to Lot's wife: she stopped moving during the battle and became a pillar of salt (Gen. 19:26). Remember what 2 Timothy 1:7 says: "God did not give us a spirit of timidity or cowardice or fear, but [He has given us a spirit] of power and of love and of sound judgment and personal discipline [abilities that result in a calm, well-balanced mind and self-control]."

In 2020 a demonic attack took my eyesight. That has happened several times, starting in 1997—even to the point that I was registered with the New York State Commission for the Blind. In 2020 not only did I lose my eyesight, but at 7:02 p.m. on December 31 of that same year, my twenty-nine-year-old sister passed away.

Hell sunk its claws into me. Within a month and a half I had two major eye surgeries. Even then my vision was not normal, and I received multiple injections in one eye. I remember sitting in the doctor's office during one of the most important checkups of my life. I was there to learn how the last surgery turned out and whether my eyesight would ever be restored. The devil tried to destroy me with torment. He distorted

God's character and manipulated my mind. He fed me thoughts about how the doctor would walk in any minute with bad news.

I had two choices: I could shrivel up and die spiritually, or I could be powerful in spiritual warfare. I decided to put on Christ and my spiritual armor and fight in the name of Jesus, with the fire of the Holy Spirit. I told myself, "I will live and not die spiritually. I will declare the works of the Lord." (See Psalm 118:17.) I made up my mind to continue doing life in Jesus. There would be no "parole." I would live out my days on "death row" as an arrow in God's quiver. By the power of the Holy Spirit, I would rise up from the ashes of satanic torment, and I would make Jesus Christ proud that He picked me. When the doctor walked into the office, he would know that I had been with Jesus, and he would deliver a praise report instead of bad news. If Jesus was with me, who could be against me? (See Romans 8:31.) If Jesus had blessed me, no devil could stand before me.

That very moment, the doctor walked in and said that in his entire career he had never completed a more elegant surgery. I said, "Doctor, let me correct you. You completed the most anointed surgery of your lifetime, in the mighty name of Jesus Christ."

My Jewish doctor looked at me with wide-open eyes. He didn't even know what to say.

So I said, "Have a blessed day, doctor." I was on my way to my victory, in Jesus' name.

That is what separates the saints from the ain'ts. I don't say that to make light of anybody's situation. People go through some terrible battles in this life. But it is time to grab the devil by the throat and be a champion in Christ Jesus.

FASTING DESTROYS DEMONIC WEAPONS

To be powerful in spiritual warfare, we need a life of fasting. Why? Because it opens prison doors. We know that Moses fasted for forty days. Jesus fasted for forty days and forty nights in the wilderness. When Saul (who became the apostle Paul) was converted, he fasted for three days. Later, when he and his shipmates were facing shipwreck, the crew went without food for several days before an angel appeared to Paul, letting him know their lives would be spared. (See Exodus 34:28, Matthew 4:2,

Acts 9:9, and 27:21–36.) If you are facing spiritual shipwreck in your walk, fasting will release you from the bonds of spiritual incarceration. Also, fasting is a lethal weapon in the Spirit against the devil, and it breaks, destroys, dismantles, and uproots demonic activity in your life a lot faster.

In a very tough season Daniel engaged in spiritual warfare by fasting for twenty-one days, and God sent reinforcements to deliver him.

> In those days I, Daniel, had been mourning for three entire weeks. I ate no tasty food, nor did any meat or wine enter my mouth; and I did not anoint (refresh, groom) myself at all for the full three weeks. On the twenty-fourth day of the first month, as I was on the bank of the great river Hiddekel [which is the Tigris], I raised my eyes and looked, and behold, there was a certain man dressed in linen, whose loins were girded with [a belt of] pure gold of Uphaz. His body also was like beryl [with a golden luster], his face had the appearance of lightning, his eyes were like flaming torches, his arms and his feet like the gleam of burnished bronze, and the sound of his words was like the noise of a multitude [of people or the roaring of the sea]. And I, Daniel, alone saw the vision [of this heavenly being], for the men who were with me did not see the vision; nevertheless, a great panic overwhelmed them, so they ran away to hide themselves. So I was left alone and saw this great vision; yet no strength was left in me, for my normal appearance turned to a deathly pale, and I grew weak and faint [with fright]. Then I heard the sound of his words; and when I heard the sound of his words, I fell on my face in a deep sleep, with my face toward the ground.
>
> Then behold, a hand touched me and set me unsteadily on my hands and knees. So he said to me, "O Daniel, you highly regarded and greatly beloved man, understand the words that I am about to say to you and stand upright, for I have now been sent to you." And while he was saying this word to me, I stood up trembling. Then he said to me, "Do not be afraid, Daniel, for from the first day that you set your heart on understanding this and on humbling yourself before your God, your words were heard, and I have come in response to your words. But the prince of the kingdom of Persia was standing in opposition to me for twenty-one days. Then, behold, Michael, one of the chief [of the

celestial] princes, came to help me, for I had been left there with
the kings of Persia."

—DANIEL 10:2–13

Fasting develops spiritual maturity. It empowers us to be victorious
and confront spiritual wickedness on every level. Obviously we also need
to live in holiness. The following scriptures make that very clear.

Who may ascend onto the mountain of the LORD? And who may
stand in His holy place? He who has clean hands and a pure
heart, who has not lifted up his soul to what is false, nor has
sworn [oaths] deceitfully. He shall receive a blessing from the
LORD, and righteousness from the God of his salvation.

—PSALM 24:3–5

The one who practices sin [separating himself from God, and
offending Him by acts of disobedience, indifference, or rebel-
lion] is of the devil [and takes his inner character and moral
values from him, not God]; for the devil has sinned and violated
God's law from the beginning. The Son of God appeared for this
purpose, to destroy the works of the devil.

—1 JOHN 3:8

The wages of sin is death, but the free gift of God [that is, His
remarkable, overwhelming gift of grace to believers] is eternal
life in Christ Jesus our Lord.

—ROMANS 6:23

It is written, "You shall be holy (set apart), for I am holy."

—1 PETER 1:16

Sin opens doors to demonic attacks. Therefore, holy living is vitally
important. That means living a pure and genuine life. None of us is perfect in any way. Even Paul admitted that. But we need to follow Paul's
example:

Not that I have already obtained it [this goal of being Christlike]
or have already been made perfect, but I actively press on so

that I may take hold of that [perfection] for which Christ Jesus took hold of me and made me His own. Brothers and sisters, I do not consider that I have made it my own yet; but one thing I do: forgetting what lies behind and reaching forward to what lies ahead, I press on toward the goal to win the [heavenly] prize of the upward call of God in Christ Jesus.

—PHILIPPIANS 3:12–14

Satan never runs short of plots and schemes. He is good at setting up spiritual barriers to keep us from living holy lives. Arsenals of satanic weapons are aimed at us for that very reason. To live a pure, dedicated, sold-out life of uncompromised holiness, we need to set our hearts and minds on Jesus Christ, from the moment we open our eyes each day until we close them and go to sleep.

FIRE PRAYERS

Lord Jesus, I renounce every demonic activity, alliance, alignment, and compromise with which I have come into agreement. Today, I am deciding in my heart to live in holiness. Let every demonic stronghold, bondage, or struggle in my life be destroyed.

Because of the cross, I am covered from the crown of my head to the soles of my feet in Christ Himself, to live a life that honors Him. May the world know that I have been with Jesus, living with purpose and godly values, aligned to His perfect will for my life.

I declare and decree that I will not depart from being the person Jesus has called me to be. By His grace, I will not be distracted, and no hindrance, delay, or blockage will be able to stop me from being and becoming who I am—a child of the King who is powerful and anointed in spiritual warfare. In the name that is above every name, the name of Jesus, amen.

Chapter 2

TEN ENTRAPMENTS THAT LEAD
TO SATANIC BONDAGE

MY HEART IS for the body of Christ. I dearly love my brothers and sisters. Whether I'm attending a conference, teaching, or praying for people in hours-long altar calls, my desire is for people to be delivered and made free in Christ. I want them to see God's best for them. That's why I share the truth about the satanic bondages that have sucker punched and entrapped so many believers. Too many people spend years trying to climb back into God's perfect will, and some never do. They just fall into the world's ways and never get out. Don't let that be your story. Read this chapter carefully. Be honest with yourself and open to anything the Holy Spirit might show you as we study these ten entrapments.

1. REJECTING AND LIVING AGAINST GOD'S PURPOSE FOR YOUR LIFE

First things first: *God is good.* He has established parameters of spiritual living to protect us from the enemy. Just as He used His Word to create the heavens and the earth (Gen. 1), He has created supernatural boundaries in the spiritual realm for us. We might not see them, but they are there. His Word and His will are established over our lives, our purpose, and our destinies.

Notice that it is *His* will, not ours. Never forget that. All protection and provision come from the word in God's mouth. When we live outside God's will, we live in satanic and demonic atmospheres. That is exactly what the devil wants, and it is his number one strategy against the church. The moment we step out of the spiritual boundaries God created, we start living in rebellion against Him and His Word.

How does that affect your life? Whether consciously or unconsciously, it takes you out of the freedom that Christ won for you and into a place of demonic bondage. Drinking the Kool-Aid of rebellion can produce only one result: satanic entrapment that ultimately leads to spiritual death.

2. INHERITING DIABOLICAL CURSES

The Bible clearly warns us in Exodus 20:5, "You shall not worship them nor serve them {meaning other gods}; for I, the LORD your God, am a jealous (impassioned) God [demanding what is rightfully and uniquely mine], visiting (avenging) the iniquity (sin, guilt) of the fathers on the children [that is, calling the children to account for the sins of their fathers], *to the third and fourth generations of those who hate Me"* (emphasis added).

Did you catch that? God visits the iniquities of previous generations on their children—not just their own children but their children's children, three and four generations down the line. Many times we believers don't realize that our children may be under generational curses inherited from our parents, grandparents, great-grandparents, and so on. These curses can come from either side of the bloodline and family tree, all the way back to Adam and Eve. If we don't deal with the spiritual roots of these issues, they will repeat themselves through later generations and restart the cycle.

Abraham was an amazing man who was blessed by God. God even called him a friend (Isa. 41:8). Abraham was wealthy, by God's hand. He understood generational blessings. Those blessings are real, but so are generational curses. Although God blessed him, Abraham felt incomplete in his spirit and life, and he cried out to God for a son. He wanted to pass on his generational blessings to his own offspring. He wanted to continue his bloodline so he could leave a mark on the earth.

Many churches talk about generational blessings and how blessed we are, but almost no one puts the finger on generational curses anymore. That does not mean no one is experiencing the hindrances, delays, blockages, and distractions these curses cause in the spirit realm. People do experience them. We need to move these spiritual boulders out of the way so the spiritual water that refreshes us can also reach through our bloodlines to the generations to come.

Generational curses are easy to explain. If a parent, grandparent, or other predecessor in your bloodline made any pact, deal, or contract with demons through involvement in occult practices, séances, witchcraft, or tarot cards, those demons found a place in your family tree. No matter how many years or centuries later you came along, the curse left a demonic residue. It has to be renounced over your family, your bloodline, and whatever gateway, portal, or demonic door was opened to it. The pact or agreement must be broken, in the name of Jesus.

I strongly recommend that you write down everything you know that may have affected your family spiritually at any point in the bloodline. Ask family members for any information that might shed light, whether it involves your father, your mother, your grandparents, or more distant generations. It could be connected to adultery, idol worship, alcohol and other addictions, abortion, sickness, having children out of wedlock—any type of alignment with ungodly acts or choices. Then you can renounce whatever brought the demonic curse and break it off your lineage.

It's time to break the devil's strong arm off the family and serve him "divorce papers," once and for all.

3. Experiencing Emotional and Physical Trauma

This door is one the devil loves and knows well. When I was operating at the highest levels of the demonic kingdom, I would study the people I wanted to attack through witchcraft. That meant understanding the blueprints of their lives and learning which familiar spirits were already at work. Then I would exploit any doors of trauma (from violence, accidents, abandonment, and so on) and any emotional hindrance. My goal was to keep the doors open and add new ones so the people could never get free in those areas. What I'm telling you comes straight from the devil's playbook. Those doors need to be shut up and shut down, once and for all.

Let me share an example of how these doors are opened in our lives. I have never shared this story, but I want you to see how the enemy takes tragic moments and makes them opportunities to steal, kill, and destroy.

Many, many years ago in my B.C. life, I was a full-time driver for a prestigious delivery company that is still around today. My base station was on 42nd Street in Manhattan at the time. The station had two doors; trucks came in one door and went out the other.

After a double shift of more than twelve hours, I returned to the station and could tell that they were falling behind. Operations were way out of order, and trucks were coming and going through the same doors. They even tried squeezing two vans through one door at the same time.

One of those vans was mine, and the corner of it pinned the security guard to the wall. He was rushed to the hospital, and he passed on several days later.

I was shocked and heartbroken over the accident. And when I heard that the man died, I was traumatized. The accident kept playing in my head, again and again. After an investigation, the company's management accepted responsibility for the incident and for not following safety protocols. But their admission of fault did not keep that trauma devil from coming on me.

Trauma is a dangerous tool that demons and the devil use. Eventually the trauma demon left me, and the effects of the attack disappeared. My point is that the trauma spirit can hit you at any time, and you can deal with it only through Christ Jesus, our Lord and Savior. There is no other way.

4. Surrendering to Ungodly Coverings

Today, the body of Christ is under some very serious deceptions—I believe the greatest deceptions ever. Everybody is looking for a covering. Everyone wants to be ordained. Everybody seems to be seeking mentoring and discipleship. Many of God's people who are under demonic bondage are suffering because they have submitted to ungodly coverings from leaders who are operating in a rebellious spirit.

I am sorry to say that we often lack discernment and are not hearing from the Lord. So we submit, surrender, and devote ourselves to satanic coverings from people who are outside God's will for us. Think about any friend, pastor, or teacher who is influencing your walk or life. You might already know that God did not choose to align you with this person. Once you touch and agree on something that God has not ordained for you, the devil has a stronghold—an opportunity to destroy what God is trying to build in your life. This happens *in the church.* Obeying and serving unrighteous coverings will bring you not a blessing but only a curse.

For the sake of your spiritual walk, it is critical to seek God and stop putting yourself in harm's way spiritually. It is dangerous to align yourself with something that God has not prepared for you. It is both disobedient and unrighteous. Don't give the devil the opportunity to kill your ministry and calling. Wake up and seek God's face. Don't make a move until He answers. Don't say yes or no. Just wait on Him.

Let me give you a common example. Many times single believers of opposite sexes meet, and one says, "You're a Christian. I'm a Christian. Let's get married." They don't realize that it's a setup from the devil. You need to enter the marital covenant with the person the Lord Jesus Christ ordained for you. The fact that he or she is a Christian is not enough. You could still be unequally yoked (2 Cor. 6:14). Wherever that happens in your life, that "tree" will not bear fruit. When all is said and done, God will curse it and toss it into the fire.

5. EMBRACING WORLDLINESS

Second Corinthians 4:3–4 says, "Even if our gospel is [in some sense] hidden [behind a veil], it is hidden [only] to those who are perishing; among them the god of this world [Satan] has blinded the minds of the unbelieving to prevent them from seeing the illuminating light of the gospel of the glory of Christ, who is the image of God."

Satan is called "the god of this world" (2 Cor. 4:4). That means he owns, controls, and has great influence over humanity, social media, and television (including fake news, politics, corrupt music, entertainment, movies, and so on). It boggles my mind to see believers staring at the one-eyed monster called *television* and watching shows that blaspheme God's name. They have become numb to the offense. It happens to all of us. But if someone were to curse our mothers, we'd be up in arms. What a shame that we lack spiritual discernment and are not grieved enough to turn off the TV or change the channel.

Before I became a full-time minister, I worked for a cheesecake maker whose cakes were the best in New York City. She was a Jewish woman, and from time to time, she would tell me how she hated Germany because of the Holocaust. She also told me to my face that she hated the name of Jesus. Believe me when I tell you how badly I needed that job. I worked on Mondays, Wednesdays, and Fridays, and that paycheck was like gold to me. But as desperate as I was, I told that lady, "I understand the Holocaust, and my heart breaks for the Jewish people. But I'm going to say one thing to you. Be careful how you come across. If you blaspheme the name of Jesus right in my face, I will walk out of here and never come back." I took a stand to honor and respect the name that is above every name. That was and is my conviction.

One of the things the enemy understands perfectly is that anything illegal has his name on it. He established demonic world systems so human beings could be made subject to them. It's sad to see Christians professing Christ and living in bondage to alcohol, drugs, and other things because their tastes are still carnal. They name Jesus but cater to their appetites. They live double lives and are just trying to "make it into heaven."

Today the culture is in bed with same-sex marriages, homosexuality, lesbianism, pornography, and abortion. We can and should pray for people who are held captive by these issues, but we are not to come into agreement with what the world is pushing. I have seen churches displaying flags that endorse homosexuality. Some churches have no problem with abortion. It might look as if they are trying to do the right thing, but they are standing as enemies of God. Do not swallow or even taste the world's poison. Proverbs 14:12 says, "There is a way which seems right to a man and appears straight before him, but its end is the way of death."

6. Owning Cursed Objects

The last thing you want to own is a cursed object. I don't care if it's worth millions; let it go. Become sensitive to things that are linked to darkness. Meditate on the following scriptures; they are very clear about darkness and light.

> So do not participate or even associate with them [in the rebelliousness of sin]. For once you were darkness, but now you are light in the Lord; walk as children of Light [live as those who are native-born to the Light] (for the fruit [the effect, the result] of the Light consists in all goodness and righteousness and truth).
>
> —Ephesians 5:7–9

> Do not love the world [of sin that opposes God and His precepts], nor the things that are in the world. If anyone loves the world, the love of the Father is not in him.
>
> —1 John 2:15

Owning a cursed object is like having a nail ready for your spiritual coffin. A cursed object is something consecrated and dedicated to demonic forces. It has demon attachments. It might be a necklace, picture, or statue. It could be a rabbit's foot, as harmless as that seems. Not everything cute is harmless, and not everything shiny is gold.

Let's not live in ignorance. Satanic bondage is lurking at your door, and when you give the enemy leeway, it will pounce. Well-meaning people who have gone on mission trips have brought home satanic objects. Often they receive or purchase them from locals who have prayed over them and washed them in animal blood. The missionaries bring them home without thinking about the articles' history, only to see their marriages or children destroyed and their callings or ministries brought down.

We've all seen people wearing T-shirts with satanic symbols. Some have dedicated themselves and given allegiance to the enemy, making pacts and agreements with whatever their shirts represent. Many people watch Harry Potter movies, *Child's Play* (Chucky) movies, or other horror movies, thinking it's no big deal. But listen, these movies introduce major curses into your home, life, walk, purpose, and destiny with the Lord Jesus Christ. They are spiritually contaminating.

You will never live in the peace and joy of the Lord if you give place to cursed objects. It's time to cut the rope and toss those things where they belong—in the trash. Remove them once and for all. Renounce them completely and fully, and don't give the devil any right to use them against you.

Beloved, imagine if Jesus Christ were an inspector. How would He respond to the items in your closet? I'm not trying to be a Pharisee about this, but I know the demonic ropes. I know which objects the devil can use to make you his spiritual puppet. People wear charms and crystals. Some burn incense in their homes and have the audacity to call it holy. It is not holy but *unholy*.

Even the words that come out of our mouths have demonic implications. Proverbs 18:21 says, "Death and life are in the power of the tongue, and those who love it and indulge it will eat its fruit and bear the consequences of their words." Instead of saying we are blessed, we say, "I'm lucky." Worldly expressions like that bring mixture into our walk. I choose to say that I'm highly favored by God. Instead of saying, "Wish me luck," I'll say, "Please pray a blessing over me."

The point is to never give the devil a chance to contaminate who you are or what God has entrusted to you. Jesus Christ has given you holy ground. There's no room there for anything but Him.

7. NOT PAYING TITHES AND THEREFORE ROBBING GOD

This subject always turns some people upside down because of the fake doctrines or false theologies they entertain about whether they should give God what belongs to Him. The truth is that not tithing brings a curse on your finances.

This issue affects many people I deeply love. I long to see them prosper so we can further the kingdom of Jesus Christ on the earth. God entrusts us with our finances. I believe the Bible points to a transfer of wealth in the end-time when it says that "the wealth of the sinner is stored up for [the hands of] the righteous" (Prov. 13:22). My prayer is for you to be in God's perfect will so you can receive the blessing when the time comes. Then you can use it with a godly mentality to further ministries and missionaries, help build churches, and help the poor and hungry as the Holy Spirit leads.

People have many questions about tithing. I have one for you: If under the Old Testament, people tithed 10 percent, how much more should we bless God as people who live under grace? Perhaps the greatest lie from the devil is one that many ministers and other believers accept: the idea that tithing originated in the Old Testament; therefore, we New Testament people don't have to tithe.

That is a false and satanic manipulation. Jesus Christ never canceled tithing in the New Testament Scriptures. Do you want to submit to a doctrine of devils? Are you OK with propaganda being spread all over the body of Christ, telling people to rob God because tithing is an "outdated" law? I believe that those who submit themselves to this falsehood are opening the door to a poverty spirit, which is a curse.

So out of obedience and your love for God, bring your tithes to His house every week. Minister to Him with them. Don't let Satan deceive you. God is your provider. He owns "the cattle on a thousand hills" (Ps. 50:10). You are in partnership with Him to build a kingdom on the earth. Don't let a poverty spirit destroy you. Inherit a blessing that will help the church at large and the kingdom of the Lord Jesus Christ in this life. In Jesus' name, amen.

8. HARBORING UNFORGIVENESS

Unforgiveness may be the deadliest poison in the world and the body of Christ. It causes a slow, spiritual death, like falling into quicksand. Only one person can throw you a rope and pull you out: the Lord Jesus Christ. Yet many of us reject that rope and keep sinking.

How is it that we believers have sinned, cried out to God, and been forgiven, yet we refuse to forgive others? Why can't we forgive our neighbors, brothers, sisters, spouses, and parents? I am not taking lightly anything that has happened to you. I have heard many tragic stories during altar calls. Sometimes I have to hold back tears hearing what my brothers and sisters in the faith have endured. Some have been molested, raped, or betrayed. They have experienced the deepest wounds a human being can experience. Now they struggle with unforgiveness.

The Son of God knows their suffering. He hung on the cross and died, disfigured to the point where He was unrecognizable. They hung Him there like a criminal, yet He gave us the greatest example of forgiveness. He said, "Father, forgive them; for they do not know what they are doing" (Luke 23:34).

Jesus showed us how to forgive. Mark 11:25–26 says, "Whenever you stand praying, if you have anything against anyone, forgive him [drop the issue, let it go], so that your Father who is in heaven will also forgive you your transgressions and wrongdoings [against Him and others]. [But if you do not forgive, neither will your Father in heaven forgive your transgressions.]" You can believe the devil's lies and stay in bondage, or you can trust the Lord Jesus Christ and forgive others.

There is another amazing Bible story about forgiveness. Look into it the way you look into a mirror. Let the Lord show you what you need to see:

> Peter came to Him {Jesus} and asked, "Lord, how many times will my brother sin against me and I forgive him and let it go?

Up to seven times?" Jesus answered him, "I say to you, not up to seven times, but seventy times seven.

"Therefore the kingdom of heaven is like a king who wished to settle accounts with his slaves. When he began the accounting, one who owed him 10,000 talents was brought to him. But because he could not repay, his master ordered him to be sold, with his wife and his children and everything that he possessed, and payment to be made. So the slave fell on his knees and begged him, saying, 'Have patience with me and I will repay you everything.' And his master's heart was moved with compassion and he released him and forgave him [canceling] the debt. But that same slave went out and found one of his fellow slaves who owed him a hundred denarii; and he seized him and began choking him, saying, 'Pay what you owe!' So his fellow slave fell on his knees and begged him earnestly, 'Have patience with me and I will repay you.' But he was unwilling and he went and had him thrown in prison until he paid back the debt. When his fellow slaves saw what had happened, they were deeply grieved and they went and reported to their master [with clarity and in detail] everything that had taken place. Then his master called him and said to him, 'You wicked and contemptible slave, I forgave all that [great] debt of yours because you begged me. Should you not have had mercy on your fellow slave [who owed you little by comparison], as I had mercy on you?' And in wrath his master turned him over to the torturers (jailers) until he paid all that he owed. My heavenly Father will also do the same to [every one of] you, if each of you does not forgive his brother from your heart."

—MATTHEW 18:21–35

Do you see your reflection in that parable? I see mine! God has forgiven us of so much. People have done us wrong, but God has forgiven us of much more. Reflect on the comparison between what you have been forgiven of and what you cannot seem to forgive. Would you rather give an ear to the devil than give your heart to the Lord Jesus Christ?

For me, one of the greatest forgiveness stories is from Joseph's life. We know what his family put him through and how horribly his brothers mistreated him. (See Genesis 37.) But I hang my hat on what Joseph said when he met his brothers for the second time. Allow me to paraphrase it: What the devil meant for evil, God turned around for good (Gen. 50:20).

That is beautiful. Joseph forgave his brothers and embraced them. Sometime later he reunited with his father, Jacob, and never said a word about what his brothers had done to him. Joseph mastered *total forgiveness*. Romans 8:37 says that "in all these things we are more than conquerors and gain an overwhelming victory through Him who loved us [so much that He died for us]." Forgiveness is victory.

9. MIXING THE WORLD WITH CHRIST: SEARCH YOUR HEART, SEARCH YOUR MIND

Is there any mixture in your life today? Do you have one foot in the world and one in church? Is one foot in bed with the enemy and the other in the holy of holies? The Bible tells us to avoid the paths of the ungodly and keep our feet on solid ground. (See Proverbs 1:15–16.) That means we need to choose where we stand.

Spiritually where are you standing right now? It might be time to do some spiritual homework and find out. If you were to grade yourself, what would your grade be? Would you give yourself an A? An F? Something in between? Are you ready to be transparent? I know you're human. I know you're a work in progress. I am too. But don't use that as an excuse. You can't just say, "Well, God knows where I'm at. He understands." You and I need to judge ourselves honestly.

Here are the ultimate questions: "Is Christ my Lord and Savior? Is He pleased with how I'm living in this season?" We all have struggles, and we all make mistakes. But is there mixture in your lifestyle? Does some of it point to the world or the devil instead of Christ? Is it your speech or some other aspect of the way you're living? Is it the condition of your mind? Is it carnal?

Whatever the issue might be, it is time to purify the vessel that God wants to live in and call holy. It's time to renounce, break, destroy, dismantle, and uproot objects, words, mindsets, demonic connections, and mediocre, lukewarm Christianity. It is time to disconnect from any dead church that you attend. Figure out where your loopholes are—you know, the areas in which you have made the enemy comfortable and the Lord Jesus Christ uncomfortable.

This is not my chance to point the finger. I am approaching this from a broken heart because I'm asking myself the same questions. When I ask the Holy Spirit to search within me, I might end up saying, "Ouch," instead of, "Hallelujah." But I want to be free, and I think you do too. So serve the devil notice and say, "You don't live here anymore."

This is about Jesus Christ and your life as a full-time believer and follower. Take to heart what Jesus told His disciples: "If anyone wishes to follow Me [as My disciple], he must deny himself [set aside selfish interests], and take up his cross daily [expressing a willingness to endure whatever may come] and follow Me [believing in Me, conforming to My example in living and, if need be, suffering or perhaps dying because of faith in Me]" (Luke 9:23).

10. Lacking Spiritual Consistency

Spiritual consistency involves following through and finishing what you started. To be spiritually consistent means to focus on what is happening not in the natural realm but in the spiritual realm. That requires discernment and patience. I don't believe that every instance of spiritual warfare ends with the enemy being knocked out in the first round. Sometimes God wants us to go through a process that helps us develop the spiritual consistency we lack.

Here is a great example of spiritual consistency from the Word of God:

> Then He spoke a parable to them, that men always ought to pray and not lose heart, saying: "There was in a certain city a judge who did not fear God nor regard man. Now there was a widow in that city; and she came to him, saying, 'Get justice for me from my adversary.' And he would not for a while; but afterward he said within himself, 'Though I do not fear God nor regard man, yet because this widow troubles me I will avenge her, lest by her continual coming she weary me.'"
>
> Then the Lord said, "Hear what the unjust judge said. And shall God not avenge His own elect who cry out day and night to Him, though He bears long with them? I tell you that He will avenge them speedily. Nevertheless, when the Son of Man comes, will He really find faith on the earth?"
>
> —Luke 18:1–8, nkjv

In the forest, you can't take one swipe at a tree with your axe and expect it to fall. Unless you keep chopping, the thing will not come down. The same is true in the spirit realm. We sometimes pray about certain issues for a couple of days or a week. Then, if God doesn't show up by Thursday, we quit. We don't realize that days, weeks, or months away from the promised land, we have given up the fight.

It's time we stopped putting Jesus Christ on the time clock. We need to walk out our faith with the spiritual consistency the Holy Spirit gives us so we can get to the other side. That means not giving up before the victory comes. It means continuing to trust the Lord Jesus Christ, walking with Him and praying it through until He releases the victory.

I have been there many times, and I thank God that the fight wasn't a quick knockout. Going through the process made me a stronger, better, and more powerful believer—and a more mature one at that. Let that be your story. You won't regret it.

Father, in Jesus' name, I renounce and break demonic ties, alignments, hindrances, delays, blockages, distractions, and every generational curse against me and my family. Father, we renounce them, completely and fully. Lord, I thank You for Your great mercy and incredible love in setting me free. In Jesus' name, amen.

Chapter 3

BIBLICAL WEAPONS SATAN AND HIS DEMONS HATE TO FACE

THE TEN ENTRAPMENTS that lead to satanic bondage are real, but God did not leave us helpless. He has prepared us with many spiritual weapons in what I call the arsenals of heaven. I believe they are meant for us to use and also live by. God provided them so we could stand on life's battlefield and guard *everything* He has given us. When we use them, we can fight the good fight and make Jesus Christ proud that He picked us for the battle.

We need to understand that spiritual warfare involves standing in green pastures one day and the valley of the shadow of death the next. Yet we don't have to fear any evil. The love and presence of God will cast out all fear (1 John 4:18; Ps. 23:4). We just need to remember that *God is with us.*

The devil, his kingdom, and his demons have their weapons, but we have weapons of mass destruction that take down their dark forces in the spirit realm. It is time to rise up, put on our armor, and shake off every hindrance, delay, blockage, distraction, doubt, and fear. It's time to show the devil and his kingdom that he knocked on the wrong doors and is messing with the wrong Christians. Like a thief who breaks into the wrong home and pays the price, the devil will pay for coming after God's own. What the devil meant for evil, the Lord Jesus Christ is going to turn around for good.

The spiritual arsenals from heaven in this chapter are yours to use against the powers of darkness on the battlefield, including in your prayer closet. One of the best things you can do is be mindful all day, every day of who King Jesus is in your life and who you are in Him. This awareness brings spiritual unity, alignment, positioning, and leverage. The devil might hit you, but he won't be able to move you. Satan and his demons hate heaven's weapons because they can destroy his kingdom and his tricks.

WEAPON 1: THE WORD OF GOD

Jeremiah 23:29 asks, "Is not My word like fire [that consumes all that cannot endure the test]...and like a hammer that breaks the [most stubborn] rock [in pieces]?" Ephesians 6:17 reminds us to "take the helmet of salvation, and the sword of the Spirit, which is the Word of God." What could be more powerful than what God says? He created the universe with His words. "{God} shakes the earth out of its place, and its pillars tremble; {He} commands the sun, and it does not shine" (Job 9:6–7).

The best example of speaking God's Word to the enemy is when Jesus answered Satan's temptation in the wilderness (Matt. 4:1–11). He didn't answer out of fear or anger. He did not try to impress the devil with His spiritual power. He simply quoted the Scriptures. (See Deuteronomy 6:13, 16; 8:3.) That was the end of that conversation. The spiritual battle was over, so Satan "left Him until a more opportune time" (Luke 4:13).

WEAPON 2: THE NAME OF JESUS

The name of Jesus establishes the authority of the One who sits at the Father's right hand. In His name, we fight from the third heaven in all authority and victory. The devil is under our feet, in the second and first heavens and underground. We don't engage the enemy in our own names. We engage in Jesus' name—the highest name of all.

Nothing can explain the power of Jesus' name better than this:

> For this reason also [because He obeyed and so completely humbled Himself], God has highly exalted Him and bestowed on Him the name which is above every name, so that at the name of Jesus every knee shall bow [in submission], of those who are in heaven and on earth and under the earth, and that every tongue will confess and openly acknowledge that Jesus Christ is Lord (sovereign God), to the glory of God the Father.
>
> —PHILIPPIANS 2:9–11

It is sad to say that many churches have removed the Word of God and the name of Jesus from their language, teaching, and preaching. How can God's people be victorious without them? They are the weapons God gave us to reach the promised land of our purpose and destiny.

WEAPON 3: THE BLOOD OF JESUS

Unfortunately many churches have also removed the blood of Jesus from their versions of the gospel. But without Jesus' blood, there is no gospel. The blood of Jesus represents the finished work of the cross and the destruction of the devil's kingdom.

Revelation 12:11 reminds us that our believing brothers and sisters "overcame and conquered {the accuser} because of the blood of the Lamb and because of the word of their testimony, for they did not love their life and renounce their faith even when faced with death." If we want to be equipped for every battle, we need to always remember the blood of the Lamb. Without it our faith is empty.

WEAPON 4: SPEAKING IN TONGUES

Speaking in tongues is a very powerful weapon that strengthens our inner beings in spiritual warfare. "One who speaks in an unknown tongue does not speak to people but to God....He speaks mysteries [secret truths, hidden things]....One who speaks in a tongue *edifies* himself" (1 Cor. 14:2, 4, emphasis added). *Edify* means "to instruct...uplift...enlighten, inform."[1] Tongues is a heavenly language that uplifts and informs us with heavenly input.

When I become spiritually exhausted praying at an altar call, I take a moment to speak in tongues. I do it to renew my strength, mind, and spirit and to refresh my anointing. Then I get back on the battlefield to go deeper and destroy every demonic or satanic attack coming against the person I'm praying for (and against me as I pray). Paul said it this way: "In the same way the Spirit [comes to us and] helps us in our weakness. We do not know what prayer to offer or how to offer it as we should, but the Spirit Himself [knows our need and at the right time] intercedes on our behalf with sighs and groanings too deep for words" (Rom. 8:26).

WEAPON 5: PRAYER

When we have communion with God through His Son Jesus Christ, all prayer is heaven's language. Prayer comes from relationship and intimacy with our Lord. Many today have lost that communication and those special moments in prayer with Him. It's time to get back into prayer. It doesn't have to happen in a prayer closet. Prayer is communion and conversation with God throughout your day, wherever you are.

Prayer also involves the church as a community. James 5:16 says, "Confess your sins to one another [your false steps, your offenses], and pray for one another, that you may be healed and restored. The heartfelt and persistent prayer of a righteous man (believer) can accomplish much [when put into action and made effective by God—it is dynamic and can have tremendous power]."

WEAPON 6: PRAISE AND WORSHIP

When I was a younger Christian reading the Old Testament, the stories of the Israelites going to battle blew my mind. I grew up in the ghettos of New York City. When gangs went out to fight, they always brought their best weapons: guns, knives, bats, and chains. They had it all. But in the Bible, God's chosen people went to battle with the worship team out front. I would have said, "Oh no! They're going to end up getting killed. They have no guns, no bats, and no chains." From my perspective, they could only be crushed. But there is something in the spirit that drives the devil and his cronies crazy and even delusional—it's praise and worship. The devil knows that heaven moves on your behalf when you are praising and worshipping God.

I remember a point in my life when I felt broken and destroyed by people I trusted, respected, and loved. It hit me so hard spiritually that for months I had no desire to read the Word of God. Yet there was something about praise and worship. Certain songs carried me through and out of that dark time. Praising and worshipping the King of kings and Lord of lords set me free.

King Jehoshaphat went through a dark season when it seemed that Judah would be crushed by its enemies. Then Jahaziel prophesied, and Jehoshaphat acted on the word of the Lord. "He appointed those who sang to the LORD and those who praised Him in their holy (priestly) attire, as they went out before the army and said, 'Praise and give thanks to the LORD, for His mercy and lovingkindness endure forever.' When they began singing and praising, the LORD set ambushes against the sons of Ammon, Moab, and Mount Seir, who had come against Judah; so they were struck down [in defeat]" (2 Chron. 20:21–22). The spoil of battle were "more than they could carry away; so much that they spent three days gathering" it (v. 25).

Weapon 7: Pulling Down the Devil's Schemes

James 4:7 says to "resist the devil [stand firm against him] and he will flee from you." Do not sit with him. Don't invite him to have coffee, tea, or milk and cookies. Cut off every conversation or dream that the devil wants you to entertain so he can infiltrate you. Cut it off completely and fully.

Many of my brothers and sisters build up the devil's schemes by continuing to talk about them. They don't realize that they are cultivating them. Don't help the devil succeed. He's trying to destroy your life, purpose, and destiny. Stop giving him an edge. It is time to renounce and resist what he is doing.

Remember what 2 Corinthians 10:3–4 says: "Though we walk in the flesh [as mortal men], we are not carrying on our [spiritual] warfare according to the flesh and using the weapons of man. The weapons of our warfare are not physical [weapons of flesh and blood]. Our weapons are divinely powerful for the destruction of fortresses."

Weapon 8: Decreeing

In Job 22, Job's friend Eliphaz said that when you "remove unrighteousness far from your tents...you will also decide and decree a thing, and it will be established for you" (vv. 23, 28). Matthew 16:19 says, "I will give you the keys (authority) of the kingdom of heaven; and whatever you bind [forbid, declare to be improper and unlawful] on earth will have [already] been bound in heaven, and whatever you loose [permit, declare lawful] on earth will have [already] been loosed in heaven."

We need to declare and decree things over our lives. Proverbs 18:21 tells us that "death and life are in the power of the tongue, and those who love it and indulge it will eat its fruit and bear the consequences of their words." We can speak life into our circumstances and situations. We can speak life into our purpose and destiny. We can speak life on the battlefield, no matter what we are going through.

There is an amazing moment in the creation story when the earth is empty, void, and dark. Then God speaks, and there is light (Gen. 1:2–3). Let that encourage you to speak to any place or season in your life that is dark. Speak to any strongholds and bondages. Declare and decree God's Word over them to loose them and bind those devils once and for all. That is how we win.

Remember what Jesus said to His disciple: "You are Peter, and on this rock I will build My church; and the gates of Hades (death) will not overpower it [by preventing the resurrection of the Christ]" (Matt. 16:18). We are His church, and the resurrection happened!

WEAPON 9: THE FIRE OF GOD AND GOD'S JUDGMENT

Hebrews 12:29 says that "our God is [indeed] a consuming fire." It's time to lay out the devil and his filthy demons by putting the fire and judgment of God on them, their kingdom, and their entrapments, plots, schemes, and setups. Look at how Elijah called down fire from heaven:

> Now Moab rebelled against Israel after the death of Ahab. Ahaziah [the king of Israel] fell through the lattice (grid) in his upper chamber which was in Samaria, and became sick [from the injury]. So he sent messengers, saying to them, "Go, inquire of Baal-zebub, the god of Ekron, if I will recover from this sickness." But the angel of the LORD said to Elijah the Tishbite, "Arise, go up to meet the messengers of the king of Samaria, and say to them, 'Is it because there is no God in Israel that you are going to inquire of Baal-zebub, the god of Ekron?' Therefore this is what the LORD says: 'You [Ahaziah] will not leave the bed on which you lie, but you will certainly die.'" So Elijah departed.
>
> When the messengers returned to Ahaziah, he said to them, "Why have you returned [so soon]?" They replied, "A man came up to meet us and said to us, 'Go, return to the king who sent you and tell him, "Thus says the LORD: 'Is it because there is no God in Israel that you send to inquire of Baal-zebub, the god of Ekron? Therefore you will not leave the bed on which you lie, but you will certainly die.'"'" The king asked them, "What was the appearance of the man who came up to meet you and said these things to you?" They answered him, "He was a hairy man with a

[wide] leather band bound around his loins." And Ahaziah said, "It is Elijah the Tishbite."

Then the king sent to Elijah a captain of fifty with his fifty [fighting men to seize the prophet]. And he went up to him, and behold, he was sitting on the top of a hill. And the captain said to him, "Man of God, the king says, 'Come down.'" Elijah replied to the captain of fifty, "So if I am a man of God, then let fire come down from heaven and consume you and your fifty [fighting men]." Then fire fell from heaven and consumed him and his fifty.

—2 KINGS 1:1–10

Every stronghold and every bondage will burn to the ground, never to rise again, in the mighty name of Jesus Christ.

WEAPON 10: FASTING

In chapter 1 you saw the power of fasting in being holy, and I shared the examples of Daniel and others. Now let's look at the example Jesus set for us with fasting.

Then Jesus was led by the [Holy] Spirit into the wilderness to be tempted by the devil. After He had gone without food for forty days and forty nights, He became hungry. And the tempter came and said to Him, "If You are the Son of God, command that these stones become bread." But Jesus replied, "It is written and forever remains written, 'Man shall not live by bread alone, but by every word that comes out of the mouth of God.'"

Then the devil took Him into the holy city [Jerusalem] and placed Him on the pinnacle (highest point) of the temple. And he said [mockingly] to Him, "If You are the Son of God, throw Yourself down; for it is written, 'He will command His angels concerning You [to serve, care for, protect and watch over You]'; and 'They will lift you up on their hands, so that You will not strike Your foot against a stone.'"

Jesus said to him, "On the other hand, it is written and forever remains written, 'You shall not test the Lord your God.'"

Again, the devil took Him up on a very high mountain and showed Him all the kingdoms of the world and the glory [splendor, magnificence, and excellence] of them; and he said to Him, "All these things I will give You, if You fall down and worship me." Then Jesus said to him, "Go away, Satan! For it is written and forever remains written, 'You shall worship the Lord your God, and serve Him only.'" Then the devil left Him; and angels came and ministered to Him [bringing Him food and serving Him].

—MATTHEW 4:1–11

We can rest assured that Jesus was intentional about fasting and about His whole wilderness experience. The devil tried every trick he knew to get Jesus to bow His knee, but Jesus was wise to him. I believe one of the lessons here is that fasting sensitizes us to what is happening in the spirit realm, where the real battle is. When Jesus' disciples were unable to deliver a man's demonized son from torment, Jesus said, "This kind of demon does not go out except by prayer and fasting" (Matt. 17:21). In other words, the disciples were unprepared for the situation.

Fasting is an incredible weapon. Please understand that it's not something I enjoy, but I do it—first, because I love God; second, because it's rewarding; and third, because it brings faster spiritual results against the enemy and his kingdom. I'm just being transparent. I need fasting. It pleases God and brings the carnal man, the flesh, and the world into alignment. It breaks the appetite for ungodly things and leaves the devil no opportunity to control me or own anything about me spiritually.

I understand that some people cannot fast for long periods. But if you can do some level of fasting, even intermittently, God will honor that. Let it become a lifestyle so you can increase the effectiveness of your spiritual warfare. The devil will have no choice but to retreat, in Jesus' mighty name.

Father, in Jesus' name—the mighty name of Jesus Christ—I thank You for the weapons of my warfare. You have made me armed and dangerous to destroy the enemy's evil plots, wiles, and schemes. Today, I declare my victory. As for me and my house, we will serve Jesus Christ all the days of our lives (Josh. 24:15). I celebrate this deliverance in His mighty name. Amen.

Chapter 4

THREE SPIRITUAL PRINCIPLES TO BE A CHAMPION IN SPIRITUAL WARFARE

WHAT IS GOD's will for you on the spiritual battlefield? I believe it's for you to win all the time, all day, every day. Jesus came to destroy *all* the works of the enemy. Scripture says, "The one who practices sin [separating himself from God, and offending Him by acts of disobedience, indifference, or rebellion] is of the devil [and takes his inner character and moral values from him, not God]; for the devil has sinned and violated God's law from the beginning. The Son of God appeared for this purpose, to destroy the works of the devil" (1 John 3:8).

The Son intended for His entire body (the church) to have abundant life (John 10:10). That is part of why Jesus spilled His blood. It breaks the satanic powers of darkness, stops the destroyer in his tracks, and enables us to recover everything the devil steals related to our purpose and destiny. God is the restorer of everything the locust has eaten. (See Joel 2:25.) His blood settled the score so we could be champions in Him.

To be victorious in spiritual warfare and experience breakthroughs in our lives, we need to understand three key principles or rules. Let's take a look.

1. DEVELOP THE CHARACTERISTICS OF A TRUE CHAMPION IN CHRIST

A champion in Christ understands spiritual discernment, has spiritual awareness and sensitivity, has the language of heaven, has heaven's arsenals on standby, understands the authority that God gave him or her, carries an anointing, and walks with the presence of God. A champion walks with the truth of Jesus Christ wrapped around his or her heart. John 8:32 tells us, "You will know the truth [regarding salvation], and the truth will set you free [from the penalty of sin]."

Walking as a champion for Jesus requires total repentance because every unconfessed sin gives legal grounds for Satan to operate in your life. You could say he owns real estate in your walk with God. True repentance does not mean you cry and fall on your face. It means you turn away from your sin—from the world's ways, from compromise, from all mixture and lukewarmness—and never go back, spiritually or naturally. You break the powers of darkness completely and fully.

2. BE FILLED WITH THE HOLY SPIRIT

Be filled with the Holy Spirit, from the crown of your head to the soles of your feet. That is the mark of a champion. I'll explain what I mean by "being filled," but first let me share a story from when I was a member of Times Square Church in New York City (which I was part of for a very long time).

One night when I was volunteering for the church's security ministry, the elder in charge of that ministry asked if I would like to walk David Wilkerson home. I was the newest volunteer on the security team, so I was shocked and awed that he would ask me. But I thank God that he did. I said, "Yes, absolutely. I would love to."

I met Pastor Dave backstage after he was done preaching. We left through a side exit and walked down the street. I remember it like it happened yesterday. It was a nice summer night with a cool breeze blowing. The sky was clear, and I could see the stars. I admit that as Pastor Dave and I walked together, I was very nervous.

Then Pastor Dave turned to me with his big blue eyes and began asking questions. I was amazed that we were engaged in a conversation, and because I was nervous, I stumbled over my words. At one point, we both laughed, and he said, "I didn't ask you that. I asked you *this*."

By the time we arrived at his building, Pastor Dave still did not know my testimony. Before we said our final goodbyes, I thought he would say something like, "Thank you. I'll see you tomorrow." But instead, he stared like he was looking through me spiritually. Then he blurted out these words, which forever changed my life: "I see Jesus Christ in you."

That is what I mean by being filled with the Holy Spirit. I believe it is the biggest honor that any believer can receive. When someone who doesn't know you or your testimony or how long you've been serving the Lord turns and says they see Jesus Christ in you, it says so much. I believe that the mark of a true champion is not in your flesh or your achievements but in Christ and Christ alone. It is about everything He has done for you. It is the mark of a person who has been with Jesus. I believe that Paul says it in such an elegant and unique way (my paraphrase): "Don't mess with me; I bear the marks of Jesus on my body." (See Galatians 6:17.)

Let that be your story. Be a champion for Jesus.

3. PERSEVERE

Another true mark of a champion in Christ is perseverance. The devil works diligently to carry out his demonic plans against you and me. He assigns demons that will try to steal, kill, and destroy. He sets up bondages, strongholds, and struggles as entrapments and pitfalls. He arranges diabolical attacks to hinder you. Those demons don't flinch or take time-outs. Like cobras waiting for the perfect moment to strike, demons wait for the opportunity that best suits Satan's agenda for you.

We need to be diligent too. That means persevering, no matter what. Jesus gave us an example of perseverance in this parable:

> Now Jesus was telling the disciples a parable to make the point that at all times they ought to pray and not give up and lose heart, saying, "In a certain city there was a judge who did not fear God and had no respect for man. There was a [desperate] widow in that city and she kept coming to him and saying, 'Give me justice and legal protection from my adversary.' For a time he would not; but later he said to himself, 'Even though I do not fear God nor respect man, yet because this widow continues to bother me, I will give her justice and legal protection; otherwise by continually coming she [will be an intolerable annoyance and she] will wear me out.'" Then the Lord said, "Listen to what the unjust judge says! And will not [our just] God defend and avenge His elect [His chosen ones] who cry out to Him day and night? Will He delay [in providing justice] on their behalf? I tell you that He will defend and avenge them quickly. However, when the Son of Man comes, will He find [this kind of persistent] faith on the earth?"
>
> —LUKE 18:1–8

The woman in the story was consistent, persistent, relentless, untouchable, and unmovable. Those are true marks of a champion. Those who have been with Jesus—who know Him, partner with Him, and commit to Him—will persevere. It's not about knowing *of* Him because you attend church occasionally or even every Sunday. It's about *knowing Jesus* and being *with* Him. When that is your testimony, who can curse you? If Jesus Christ has blessed you, who can unbless you?

The true mark of believers who fight the good fight is that they know they are in Him and He is in them. No matter what comes their way, they stand. They have seen too much in Jesus Christ to quit. When I look back on my walk with Him, the only footprints I see on the sand are His. I did not walk because He carried me through.[1]

Repeat these words with me: *Remember me.* In other words, every time you're in the fight, every time you're in the fire, every time the devil comes as a flood, say those simple words, just as the thief on the cross said them to Jesus, the Man in the middle: "Remember me" (Luke 23:42). Then remember Jesus. Remind yourself of all that He has done for you. Remember what He promised: *shalom*, "nothing missing, nothing broken."[2] Remember the goodness of His name and His promises. Remember His Word over your life. Then tell Him again, "Remember me," knowing that soon after the thief said those words, he found himself in eternity.

I will leave you with the words of David Wilkerson. Every time there was a spiritual drama in my life, he would say to me, "John, God knows."

David Wilkerson was a champion. And we are champions in Him who calls us by name.

> *Father, in Jesus' name, I declare and decree over my life that You have made me to be a champion, a spiritual winner, a spiritual sniper. You created me with a purpose and destiny before the foundations of the earth. I'm here to fulfill that purpose and destiny and be a champion for Jesus Christ, my Lord and Savior. Help me, Lord, to make You proud that You picked me for the spiritual-warfare fight. I declare this over my life, in the unmatchable name of Jesus Christ. Amen.*

Chapter 5

PRAYERS OF REPENTANCE

REPENTANCE IS ABOUT acknowledging your sins and correcting your course. When you repent, you make peace with God and get back into right standing with Him. Repentance means returning to God's perfect will and realizing that He always knows best.

That requires making a spiritual assessment of your bloodline on both sides of the family, realizing that sin has been passed from generation to generation, going all the way back to Adam and Eve. The point is to spiritually assess any blockages, hindrances, delays, and distractions that are "glooming and dooming" your life, home, ministry, purpose, or destiny. It means recognizing your known offenses against others and understanding that some of your offenses are still unknown to you. Repentance means acknowledging any hidden unforgiveness in your heart, no matter how minor it seems.

It is important to take an inventory of your family tree, call out whatever sin you find, and repent. The devil takes opportunity with unconfessed sin. He attacks believers from four directions, spiritually speaking: the north, south, east, and west. The north involves demonic attacks that happen in front of you and are heading directly at you. Spiritually speaking, the Lord signs off on these attacks as part of your assignment. Therefore, you can trust Him and fight the good fight. If you follow through, you will move from glory to glory. You can see this kind of frontal attack in David's life, when he went ahead and fought the giant. Killing Goliath was part of David's divine assignment, and he got the victory.

Demonic attacks from the east or west are attacks that come from the side. They include lingering issues in the spirit that the enemy uses to throw you a sucker punch. When David fought Goliath, he went straight ahead and took him down. But David was naive and ignorant about the threat from his right side, where King Saul stood. The enemy used Saul to sucker punch David, who spent several years of his life running from Saul and hiding in caves.

An attack from the south comes when the enemy approaches you from behind—in other words, from your past. He will either remind you of your past, torment you with some aspect of it, or try to convince you that your past is not behind you (which it is). If you think about the issues and attacks you face from this directional perspective, it will help you spiritually assess your history and call to repentance anything that is not from God.

FRIEND OR FOE?

I want to share something that I've never shared before about another type of attack the devil uses against you. This one masquerades as a friend—someone or something with which you have made peace. When you look behind the curtain, however, this could be the worst enemy *ever* in your walk with the Lord. Here is an example from the Book of Joshua:

> Now when all the kings who were beyond the Jordan, in the hill country and in the lowland [at the western edge of the hills of Judea], and all along the coast of the Great [Mediterranean] Sea toward Lebanon, the Hittite and the Amorite, the Canaanite, the Perizzite, the Hivite and the Jebusite, heard of this [army and its victories over Jericho and Ai], they gathered together with one purpose to fight with Joshua and with Israel.
>
> But when the people of Gibeon [the Hivites] heard what Joshua had done to Jericho and Ai, they too acted craftily and cunningly, and set out and took along provisions, but took worn-out sacks on their donkeys, and wineskins (leather bottles) that were worn out and split open and patched together, and worn-out and patched sandals on their feet, and worn-out clothes; and all their supply of food was dry and had turned to crumbs. They went to Joshua in the camp at Gilgal and said to him and the men of Israel, "We have come from a far country; so now, make a covenant (treaty) with us." But the men of Israel said to the Hivites, "Perhaps you are living within our land; how then can we make a covenant (treaty) with you?" They said to Joshua, "We are your servants." Then Joshua said to them, "Who are you, and where do you come from?" They said to him, "Your servants have come from a country that is very far away because of the fame of

the LORD your God; for we have heard the news about Him and all [the remarkable things] that He did in Egypt, and everything that He did to the two kings of the Amorites who were beyond the Jordan, to Sihon the king of Heshbon and to Og the king of Bashan who lived in Ashtaroth. So our elders and all the residents of our country said to us, 'Take provisions for the journey and go to meet the sons of Israel and say to them, "We are your servants; now make a covenant (treaty) with us."' This bread of ours was hot (fresh) when we took it along as our provision from our houses on the day we left to come to you; now look, it is dry and has turned to crumbs. These wineskins which we filled were new, and look, they are split; our clothes and our sandals are worn out because of the very long journey [that we had to make]." So the men [of Israel] took some of their own provisions [and offered them in friendship], and [foolishly] did not ask for the counsel of the LORD. Joshua made peace with them and made a covenant (treaty) with them, to let them live; and the leaders of the congregation [of Israel] swore an oath to them.

It happened that three days after they had made a covenant (treaty) with them, the Israelites heard that they were [actually] their neighbors and that they were living among them.

JOSHUA 9:1–16

This enemy was designed to be called a friend, although the "friend" could not be identified, and later proved to be a demonic spiritual cancer. Like a physical cancer that your cells and immune system cannot locate or recognize until it's too late, this spiritual cancer is an enemy within. It does damage before you identify it correctly.

As is true of everything we have discussed in this chapter, you destroy this "cancer" through repentance and self-control. Address the enemy within by first understanding what Paul confessed: "I know that nothing good lives in me, that is, in my flesh [my human nature, my worldliness—my sinful capacity]. For the willingness [to do good] is present in me, but the doing of good is not" (Rom. 7:18).

Let me give you a practical example of how this devil works. Maybe it is a situation with unhealthy food. You eat it anyway because you like it and see it as your friend. Eating it is enjoyable and gives you a sense of fulfillment. But "your body is a temple of the Holy Spirit" (1 Cor. 6:19).

Therefore, there needs to be spiritual balance in what you eat. Without that balance a demon of infirmity shows up. It might be high blood pressure, diabetes, or even heart issues. What you think is your friend becomes your worst enemy. It is designed to shorten your life, cut you off from your purpose, and destroy your destiny.

Here's another example of this type of attack: Sometimes the Holy Spirit puts a check in your spirit about a friendship or a person. If you disregard that alarm and allow the person into your circle, the demonic agenda that he or she carries out will turn your life spiritually upside down.

Personally I use the Old Testament system of the outer court, the middle court, and the holy of holies. Some people in my life will always be in the outer court. Others will enter the middle court. A few will gain access to my "holy of holies"; I can count those on one hand.

These are just a few examples of the spiritual assessments you can make to root out the spiritual enemies in your camp. It's time to repent of embracing them and give them all an eviction notice.

FIRE PRAYERS

Holy Spirit, I present my spirit, soul, and body to You now (Rom. 12:1–2), *in the name of Jesus.*

Holy Spirit, I ask You to pray over me, through me, and in me (Rom. 8:26–27). *Purify me, in the unmatchable name of Jesus Christ.*

Holy Spirit, I ask You to bring to my remembrance anything and everything I need to repent of. Help me put all of it on the altar so the fire of God can burn it completely and fully, in Jesus' name.

I come before the throne of God, where I find mercy and grace (Heb. 4:16), *and I repent of all the sins in my mind, in my heart, and in the words of my mouth (Ps. 19:14), in the name of Jesus.*

Father, in the name of Jesus, I submit myself to You completely and fully, so You can examine me (Ps. 139:23–24).

Holy Spirit, I ask You to forgive me for having grieved You in any known or unknown way, in Jesus' name.

Lord, I repent and ask Your forgiveness for having judged any brother or sister (Matt. 7:1–2), in Jesus' name.

I repent for every rebellious way in which I have dishonored the Lord Jesus Christ. Please forgive me, in Jesus' name.

Holy Spirit, I ask that You put Your finger on any area in which I have unforgiveness for anyone so I can completely and fully repent.

In Jesus' name, I repent for every time I sinned and came into agreement with the devil.

I bind every satanic power that is seen in the negative, repetitive patterns and cycles in my life. In the name of Jesus, I pray. Amen.

I curse to the root every hindrance, delay, blockage, and distraction. Let all of it shrivel up and die today, in the unmatchable name of Jesus Christ.

I release the fire of the Holy Spirit over every satanic door or gateway that I have opened, knowingly or unknowingly, that has allowed the devil to enter in any way, shape, or form to bring sin into my life. I repent in the name of Jesus.

I release the arsenals of heaven on every demon that has preyed on my mind, heart, or soul to lead me into a lifestyle of sin. In Jesus' name, amen.

Lord, forgive me for offending You, grieving You, and breaking Your heart because of my shortcomings. In Jesus' name, amen.

I come to true repentance right now. Holy Spirit, purify and sanctify me, from the crown of my head to the soles of my feet. In Jesus' name, amen.

Lord, by the power of the Holy Spirit, let my weaknesses become strengths in every area of my life. In Jesus' mighty name, amen.

Thank You, Lord Jesus, for forgiving me. I praise You and shout, "Hallelujah!"

Holy Spirit, I invite You back into my heart. I celebrate my salvation, healing, deliverance, and forgiveness, in the unmatchable name of Jesus Christ.

Chapter 6

PRAYERS OF RENUNCIATION

PRAYERS OF RENUNCIATION remove any legal grounds the enemy of your soul wants to use against you. They let him know that he has no rights over you and that any demonic contracts are dissolved. By the power of the Holy Spirit and in keeping with God's will for you, the devil must accept the eviction notice you serve and clear out of any territory you may have given him in the past.

Remember that the thief comes with destruction in mind, but Jesus comes to give you overflowing, abundant life (John 10:10). Satan has no business spiritually incarcerating you, and you have no business allowing him to do it. Be wise to him.

Before you begin the renunciations, look at three tools the devil uses progressively to set you up. When you learn to recognize them and see how he puts your name on them, you will know exactly what you need to renounce.

1. spiritual struggles

2. spiritual strongholds

3. spiritual bondage

It is shocking to me that the church is not teaching God's people about this progression. The enemy understands that before he can get you into a stronghold or into bondage, he has to bring spiritual struggles into your life. These are demonic temptations of all kinds that seem attractive, interesting, inviting, or harmless.

We can learn about the enemy's tactics in Psalm 91. Verse 3 speaks about the fowler's traps. The fowler is the devil, and his entrapments are the tools he uses against you. In verse 13 some translations mention "the young lion." Metaphorically, that represents your small struggles or small sins. Somehow we think they're no big deal. We believe we can put away our "little sins" whenever we choose. Yet we like playing with them now and again. That is called *a struggle*.

Pornography is a great example. So is marijuana. You dabble a little, and then a little more. You say you can walk away, but do you? And what about marijuana being legal? The government might say it is, but it's not legal in the kingdom of the Lord Jesus Christ. If you haven't killed the marijuana issue in your life, it is a struggle. Unless you deal with it, it will kill you spiritually at some point. It's like a cute little pit bull puppy. You can dominate it and put it in its crate whenever you want. When it's small, you have leverage and can control it. Spiritual struggles are like that. You think you can call the shots. But when the "puppy" becomes sixty pounds of solid muscle, it can bite you at will. The struggle has become a stronghold, and bondage is not far behind.

As kids many of us played with matches. It seemed fun, but as the saying goes, it can get you burned. The "fun" can lead to disaster, burning down a house and getting people killed. We grown-ups can be equally careless spiritually. The Bible warns us to "be sober [well balanced and self-disciplined], be alert and cautious at all times" because "that enemy of yours, the devil, prowls around like a roaring lion [fiercely hungry], seeking someone to devour" (1 Pet. 5:8). We cannot afford carelessness. We need to be spiritually alert.

The renunciation prayers will help you wake up and return to God's perfect will. If you're diligent, they will make a champion out of you. Praying them shames the devil and lets him know that you are not playing anymore. You are going to renounce your struggles and strongholds. And if spiritual bondage has incarcerated you, your "jail cell" will begin to open.

Renunciation works like spiritual pruning shears: it cuts the issue to its roots, and it does so in Jesus' name. So go ahead, shame the devil and make Jesus Christ proud.

FIRE PRAYERS

Listen to me, Satan, as I renounce all known and unknown spiritual agreements that I've made with your kingdom, in the name of Jesus.

I renounce and reject all satanic contracts, all legal rights, and any demonic offers that I accepted from the kingdom of darkness, the devil, or the demons. I serve them an eviction notice today, in the name of Jesus.

I renounce all lust, perversion, and immorality and every unclean, foul, wicked spirit out of my life today, in Jesus' name.

I renounce all witchcraft, sorcery, and divination; every occult practice, including tarot cards, Ouija boards, and horoscopes; or any occult involvement on any level, in Jesus' name.

I renounce all kinds of ungodly, immoral soul ties that bring shame to the name of Jesus. I command them to loose me now, in His mighty name.

Right now I renounce all hatred, anger, resentment, revenge, retribution, unforgiveness, bitterness, and anger, in the name of Jesus.

I renounce all demonic or satanic habits, temptations, and struggles that have in any way affected my spiritual life and relationship with the Lord Jesus Christ. Holy Spirit, burn all of it out of me, in Jesus' name. Amen.

I renounce pride, envy, jealousy, covetousness, the lust of the eyes, and the lust of the flesh, in the name of Jesus.

I renounce every satanic or demonic, unclean spirit of homosexual tendencies or practices, as well as any perversion, pornography, lust, or sexual relations outside marriage. I cut the rope, and I shut the door. In the name of Jesus, amen.

I renounce all ungodly covenants, oaths, and vows that I or anyone in my bloodline has made with the devil, whether on my mother's or father's side of the family. I curse them to the root. Let them shrivel up and die, in the name of Jesus.

I renounce the devil, his kingdom, his practices, and any agreements that I have made with any demons, principalities, territorial spirits, and familial spirits, in Jesus' name.

In the name of Jesus, I renounce and revoke any words that I have spoken that have given the devil legal grounds over my life.

In the name of Jesus, I renounce any evil covenants or oaths that I have made with the devil or any demon during my dreams.

I renounce all false demonic prophecies that have been spoken over me in church, by divination inside or outside the church, or by any witch operating in the spirit of the world. I break those words off me now, in Jesus' name.

Let every demonic file the devil has had against me, from birth until this moment, be burned with the fire of the Holy Spirit.

Today, I fully and completely renounce every struggle, stronghold, and bondage that has a name on it. (Call out the name of each one.) In Jesus' name, all legal grounds are now destroyed.

Let every yes that I have given the devil to access legal grounds against me be turned into a no in the fire of the Holy Spirit. In Jesus' name.

By the fire of the Holy Spirit, I renounce every hidden work of darkness in my life (Eph. 5:11). In Jesus' name, amen.

In Jesus' name, I destroy and renounce every demonic contract that is still active against me and my family, ministry, purpose, destiny, marriage, child(ren), and loved ones. Let it burn now in the fire of the Holy Spirit.

I renounce and break off every yoke of bondage, every type of stronghold, and every satanic agreement that I've made with the devil. By the blood of Jesus, I destroy them.

Holy Spirit, purify me and fill every void in my life with the blood of Jesus. Fully renew my mind, heart, spirit, and soul. I turn the page against the devil and give the pen back to You, Jesus Christ. Continue writing my story, Lord, so when my life is over, You can be proud that You picked me.

I praise You, Jesus, and I shout, "Hallelujah!" Thank You, Holy Spirit, for destroying every demonic contract that was over me. In Jesus' name, I pray. Amen.

Chapter 7

PRAYERS FOR SPIRITUAL DISCERNMENT

I N MY OPINION nothing represents Christ like the underground church in China. Those believers are reverent in their faith. In that hostile environment the day you stand up for Christ can be the day you die.

I heard an interesting story about a Chinese believer—someone I see as an ambassador of our Lord Jesus Christ—who visited America and toured several churches. When he returned to China, people asked him what had impressed him the most.

His answer knocked me over. He said, "I am amazed at how much the church in America can accomplish without the Holy Spirit."

Talk about bursting someone's balloon!

I believe in my heart that America will eventually understand his perspective. We will be tested much like China has been tested to see what we're made of. We're not there yet. Many of our churches are still confusing talent with anointed ministry. We think a church is good because it is large and the music sounds good. But that is not about the Lord. Instead of a sermon in the house of God, we are entertained by talented speakers. We swap God's presence for something that tickles our ears. We discern the voices of certain celebrities. We know the voices of our loved ones and friends. But can we distinguish the voice of the Holy Spirit? Do we have the discernment to do that?

We have come to a place where some people say, "I have to fast to hear from the Holy Spirit." If you have to fast to hear from the Holy Spirit, then you don't know His voice. Fasting is a whole different thing. You should know the voice of the Holy Spirit with or without fasting. You can hear Him when you awaken. You can hear Him at work or in a crowded market. When the Holy Spirit speaks, you can discern His voice and know that He is speaking to you. He's the One you want to hear in church.

We have missed the mark because we lack the spirit of discernment. We need to ask the Lord to give us spiritual eyes that see Him and spiritual ears that hear what the Holy Spirit is saying. This is not a put-down. It's a wake-up call for all of us who believe in Christ. It is time to pray.

Too often we don't know where the devil's attacks are coming from. He could be standing right in front of us, but we cannot discern him. He's in our blind spots, and he sucker punches us. He can do it because we lack the deep, hard-core relationship needed to hear the Holy Spirit's warnings. He will reveal the devil's position. But we have to rise up and be the vessels of honor God calls us to be. That starts with discerning the times, discerning our purpose and destiny, and, above all, discerning the Lord's voice. He will tell you what season you are in. He will show you where you are going and where you are to finish with Christ. Just ask Him. Be persistent and listen for His answer.

> Ask, and it will be given to you; seek, and you will find; knock, and it will be opened to you. For everyone who asks receives, and he who seeks finds, and to him who knocks it will be opened. Or what man is there among you who, if his son asks for bread, will give him a stone? Or if he asks for a fish, will he give him a serpent? If you then, being evil, know how to give good gifts to your children, how much more will your Father who is in heaven give good things to those who ask Him!
>
> —MATTHEW 7:7–11, NKJV

FIRE PRAYERS

Father, in the name of Jesus, please remove the blindfold from my eyes.

Holy Spirit, in Jesus' name, I ask You to remove the spiritual cataracts that are clouding my vision.

Holy Spirit, please come into my life and be my best friend, in Jesus' name.

Holy Spirit, give me eyes to see in the spirit realm and ears to hear Your voice and walk with You, all the days of my life (John 10:27; Col. 2:6).

Father, let the eyes of my understanding be enlightened (Eph. 1:18), *in Jesus' name.*

Lord, anoint my spiritual eyes to see and my spiritual ears to hear what the Holy Spirit has to say in every season of my life (John 16:13). *In Jesus' name, amen.*

Father, please reveal the things that belong to me. In Jesus' name, amen.

Father God, in the mighty name of Jesus, reveal the secrets of heaven for my life and pour them into my heart.

Holy Spirit, teach me to know Your voice, in Jesus' name.

Holy Spirit, minister to my heart, ears, and eyes so I understand the things of heaven and have revelation and clarity in my heart and spirit as I walk with You. Help me know Your voice clearly and completely (John 10:27). *In the mighty name of Jesus Christ, amen.*

Holy Spirit, let me understand the deep things of God (1 Cor. 2:10). *In the name of Jesus, amen.*

Holy Spirit, let the gift of revelation be my portion in my lifetime, in Jesus' name.

Holy Spirit, teach me how to walk and how to discern the times and the seasons that I'm in so I can complete my race with You, all the days of my earthly life (1 Chron. 12:32).

Holy Spirit, lead, guide, nourish, and protect me. Never let me lose the sound of Your voice in my ear. For all my days, let it be crystal clear. I pray this in the mighty name of Jesus Christ. Amen.

Holy Spirit, just as Paul received abundance of revelation and clarity in his spirit to see the holy things of God, let that be my portion, my purpose, and my destiny as I walk with You. Let nothing of You be cut short in my life. Help me finish my race and say, "I have fought the good fight" (2 Tim. 4:7, NIV). Let it be because I knew Your voice and discerned all that God has for me. Let that be my beginning and my end, in the unmatchable name of Jesus Christ. Amen.

Chapter 8

DECLARATIONS TO STRENGTHEN YOUR POSITION IN THE SPIRIT REALM

BASED ON GOD'S Word, I want to share with you the opportunities, blessings, and authority you have to confess, declare, and strengthen your position in the spirit realm. It's so important to understand that "death and life are in the power of the tongue, and those who love it and indulge it will eat its fruit and bear the consequences of their words" (Prov. 18:21). Whatever you confess with your mouth and believe in your heart should be established in the spirit realm.

Let that settle in your spirit. There is no room for error. It is crucial to not only understand the truth but also walk in it, accomplish it, confess it, declare it, and decree it. Romans 10:9 says, "If you confess with your mouth the Lord Jesus and believe in your heart that God has raised Him from the dead, you will be saved" (NKJV).

Think about that. Meditate on it. It is the number one key—not only to entering heaven but also to being saved and in right standing with God. If you confess and agree with God concerning your life, your relationship with Him, and your destiny, the devil won't stand a chance against you. That's why we are going to touch and agree with the Holy Spirit. We do both, because one hand cannot clap alone. Establish these confessions in the spirit realm by repeating them from your heart and saying them aloud. Let the devil hear what you say. Let the demonic kingdom understand where you are coming from. Let your words describe where you stand, where you are going, and where your finish line is in Christ.

FIRE PRAYERS

I confess that I am a child of God (Rom. 8:16).

I declare that I am born again by the Spirit of God (John 3:6).

I confess and declare that Jesus Christ has become a curse in my place; therefore, I am the righteousness of God in Christ Jesus (Gal. 3:13; 2 Cor. 5:21).

I am a citizen of the heavenly kingdom. I don't carry an earthly passport. My passport is written with the blood of Jesus, which tells where I came from and where I am going, in Jesus' name.

I confess that by the finished work of the cross, all demons and the devil himself are under my feet, in Jesus' name.

I am the head and not the tail, in Jesus' name (Deut. 28:13).

Today and forevermore, I reign and rule with Jesus Christ and am seated in heavenly places (Eph. 2:6).

Devil, I remind you that my body is a temple of the Holy Spirit (1 Cor. 6:19), in the mighty name of Jesus Christ.

I am no longer the old person with the old person's weaknesses. I am a new creation, and I can do all things through Christ Jesus, who paid a price for me and strengthens me (2 Cor. 5:17; Phil. 4:13). In His mighty, untouchable name, amen.

I declare and decree that I am blessed with all spiritual blessings in Christ Jesus (Eph. 1:3).

Today and forever, my life is hidden in Christ. Therefore, I will live and not die (Col. 3:3; Ps. 118:17). No demonic or spiritual premature event will stop me from receiving and accomplishing God's best (Ps. 91:16). In Jesus' name, amen.

Devil, I declare that I am not a mistake. I have been chosen, handpicked before the foundations of the earth (Eph. 1:4). In the mighty name of Jesus, I will be used to destroy your kingdom.

In this season and the season to come, my hope is in Christ who lives in me and cannot fail. Greater is He who lives in me than he who lives in the world (1 John 4:4). In Jesus' name, amen.

I confess that I see the goodness of the Lord in my life now, in the land of the living (Ps. 27:13). In Jesus' name, amen.

Today I declare that any satanic assignment over my life will be turned into a blessing and will prosper me to accomplish and abound in God's purpose and destiny for me. In Jesus' name, amen.

I know by the Word of God that established the heavens and the earth that I have been created to be an overcomer (1 John 4:4; 5:4–5), to triumph over every scheme and plot of the devil over my life, family, loved ones, ministry, career, job, purpose, and destiny (Rom. 8:37), in Jesus' mighty name.

Yesterday, today, and tomorrow, no weapon formed against me will prosper (Isa. 54:17). I curse to the root every demonic word against my life, my season, or my day, in Jesus' name.

By the power of Jesus' blood, I quench and destroy every demonic fiery arrow (Eph. 6:16). I send it back to the devil's camp to destroy every evil plot against me. In Jesus' name, amen.

Today I stand on the victory side of Christ's finished work, because the One who is in me is greater than the one that lives in the world (1 John 4:4).

I am anointed to accomplish, succeed in, and finish my course by the power of the Holy Spirit, who dwells in me. No evil plan, no work of the devil, no scheme of the enemy will be able to stop what God started in me (Phil. 1:6). In Jesus' name, amen.

PART II

DISRUPTING SATANIC SCHEMES

Chapter 9

THE BLOOD OF JESUS: ARSENAL PRAYERS THAT GIVE DEMONS HEART ATTACKS

THERE IS POWER—INCREDIBLE, unmatchable power—in the blood of Jesus. When sin came into the world through Adam and Eve, the devil thought he accomplished a victory. But God was way ahead of the devil, and that "victory" was bogus. The shed blood of Jesus Christ not only settled the score but also remitted our sin. He accomplished and established the victory in and through us. The finished work of the cross overcame the devil's plans.

That was the ultimate victory. It stripped the devil butt naked and defeated him and his kingdom forever. No wonder he fears the blood of Jesus. He is so terrified that he trembles and doesn't know what to do with himself.

You might ask, "Why, John?"

It's because the blood of Jesus reminds him of the agreement between the Father and the Son for humanity's redemption. It reminds him that he has been stripped to nothing and shut up in the kingdom of darkness. He knows that the blood has life: in Christ, in us, and in the kingdom of our Father who loves us. As John 3:16 says, "For God so [greatly] loved and dearly prized the world, that He [even] gave His [One and] only begotten Son, so that whoever believes and trusts in Him [as Savior] shall not perish, but have eternal life."

Jesus is "the way and the truth and the life" (John 14:6, NIV). The agreement between us and heaven has been settled. It's time to put the devil to flight and make the demons tremble and pay the price. And they will—as we pray these fire prayers. The powers of darkness in the spirit realm will quiver. Whatever they attempted to do in our lives must come down, whether it's fear, terror, sickness, or any kind of torment. The demons know that they will drown just as Pharaoh and his army drowned in the Red Sea—but this time in the powerful blood of Jesus.

Before we get to the fire prayers, repeat this prayer with me:

Father, I thank You for the blood of the Lord Jesus Christ. I have been baptized in His blood, for me and my house, my child(ren) and my family, and everything with which You have entrusted me.

Holy Spirit, as I pray the fire prayers, make me stealthy in the spirit realm so I can operate against the kingdom of darkness and whatever monitoring system it has against me. Thank You that any such system will disappear. I will accomplish my victory through the blood of Jesus Christ. Amen.

Fire Prayers

Let the blood of the cross stand between me and my past, present, and future. Let every demonic assignment of the devil be destroyed today, in Jesus' name.

By the blood of Jesus Christ, I destroy, paralyze, and conquer all demonic assignments against my purpose, destiny, family, ministry, and finances. I smite every demon's head with Jesus' blood, destroying every plot and scheme against me. I stand on the victory side of the finished work of the cross, in Jesus' name.

Let the power of the blood of Jesus Christ be released into the atmosphere around and in me, to destroy every fiery dart, every astral-projecting devil from the second and first heaven, and every demon on the ground. Let the fire of the Holy Spirit rain on them now, in Jesus' name.

Let the power of the blood of Jesus Christ release me from every form of spiritual incarceration and every incarcerating mindset in my heart, spirit, and soul. I am free now, in Jesus' name.

Let every unholy door that I have opened to the enemy, whether consciously or unconsciously, be sealed shut now, by the blood of Jesus Christ.

I stand on God's Word, covered by Jesus' blood, and I declare over my life and being, from the crown of my head to the soles of my feet, that I will be unshakable and unmovable. In the name of Jesus Christ, amen.

I soak my life, purpose, and destiny in the blood of Jesus, for today and forevermore.

Let the blood of Jesus Christ strengthen, quicken, and establish me in every area of my life. In Jesus' name, amen.

I declare the blood of Jesus Christ against every portal, gateway, and open door of demonic assignment over my life. Let it be destroyed and sealed shut forever, in Jesus' name.

Let the blood of Jesus Christ stand in front of me, beside me, and behind me as a shield against every satanic wile, plot, and scheme. I will triumph and be victorious, and I will reach my destiny, in Jesus' name.

Let every evil seed the devil has planted or will try to plant in my life be destroyed. Let it shrivel up and die, in the name of Jesus.

I apply the blood of Jesus over my house, marriage, child(ren), family, and health and over every divine opportunity in my life. In Jesus' name, amen.

Let every demonic strategy and satanic assignment against my life drown in the blood of Jesus.

I draw a line of protection around me, in me, and through me everywhere I go. No weapon formed against me will prosper (Isa. 54:17), and no devil will be able to stand in my way. In the mighty name of Jesus Christ, amen.

I curse all satanic operations of witches, warlocks, and occult devils against my destiny. I destroy them all with the blood of Jesus.

Let the fire of the Holy Spirit fall on the head of every demonic power that is trying to frustrate or stop God's plan for my life. Confuse the devil's camp, Lord. Let the demons attack one another. Release my purpose and my destiny now, in Jesus' name.

I pour the blood of Jesus over all witchcraft and every altar, assignment, plot, and scheme, as well as every devil that has been assigned to bring destruction to my life, family, ministry, purpose, destiny, and finances. I declare and decree that the arsenals of heaven will rain their power on the wicked heads in the kingdom of darkness and that they will shrivel up and die, in Jesus' name.

Let every satanic meeting of warlocks and witches in which my name is mentioned be destroyed by the blood of Jesus.

I release warring angels from Michael's quarter to destroy every demonic strategy the enemy has planned for me this year. Let it be annihilated and pulverized, never to rise up against me in any way. In Jesus' name, amen.

Father, I give You the praise and glory for what You have done in my life, both the things I know about and the things I don't. I thank You in the untouchable, all-powerful name of Jesus Christ. Amen.

Chapter 10

PRAYERS TO DESTROY SATANIC DEDICATIONS AND AGREEMENTS

DEDICATION TO THE dark side is powerful and involves loyalty and commitment. In other words, you surrender to the devil and his kingdom.

That was once my life. I was recruited at seven and a half years old when a demonic necklace fell from the second heaven. I was with a friend in a rundown lot in the South Bronx, breaking windows in abandoned buildings, when the necklace ended up at my feet. I stuck it in my pocket and thought I heard my mom's voice calling me to come home—a familial spirit was beckoning me. Without any knowledge of what I was doing, I put on the necklace and started the dedication.

When I was around eight years old, my mom and my aunt (a high-ranking witch) took me to the witch's house to get tarot card readings. That is where my journey began in earnest—strolling through the South Bronx to find the witch's house. When we arrived, I saw a place of gloom and doom. The lady's face could be described only as evil. She fixed her attention on me, and from that day until I was thirty-five, I was groomed and trained in the demonic church. In the satanic world we had services from 7 p.m. until 5 a.m., with the hierarchy gathered in the shadows of darkness. I had a demonic wedding on Halloween night. High-ranking demons, witches, and warlocks came to baptize my wedding and ceremonially (but demonically) "bless" it. For years I gave the devil my loyalty and my commitment to serve him.

Thank God for Jesus Christ, who looked my way and plucked me out of the pit of hell.

I have seen God sever satanic ties in my life. Today, you are going to break and destroy every dedication and agreement with any religious and demonic spirits, including any demonic rituals practiced in certain Christian denominations or sects and demonic rituals and dedications like the ones I lived under in purely satanic circles. These spiritual, demonic doors make you vulnerable. You will be spiritually weak and anemic until you renounce them, uproot them, and break every demonic alignment, stronghold, and bondage by the blood of Jesus Christ. Then the doors are closed, and you and your children are set free (with no iniquity transferring for the three to four generations prescribed in Deuteronomy 5:9).

THE DEVIL'S GAME

The devil's game is to make satanic dedications seem normal. They appear to offer blessings and protection, because that is how the devil (who masquerades as an angel of light) presents them. We can mistakenly excuse demonic dark practices, saying, "They are part of my culture and part of my life. My grandmother and grandfather did them. My mother and auntie did them. Now it's my turn."

That is a lie from the pit of hell.

These are setups—entrapments the devil has used for centuries. There is nothing cute about them, and you will never profit from them. You will only be bound by them. The devil will own the legal rights over your life. As long as he does, you will never be free.

Thank God for the opportunity He is giving us through His Son, Jesus Christ, to destroy satanic dedications and agreements, regardless of our ages. At seven and a half, I was ignorant. The devil loves targeting ignorant people. He knows that God's people "are destroyed for lack of knowledge" and for forgetting God's law and jeopardizing their children (Hos. 4:6). When satanic dedication occurs, the person's life is ruined. It's like a runaway train that picks up speed and eventually crashes and burns.

Before we get to the fire prayers, please meditate on the passages below. Let them remind you of who you *really* are, who Christ has made you to be, and what He stands ready to do for you.

> Christ purchased our freedom and redeemed us from the curse of the Law and its condemnation by becoming a curse for us—for it is written, "Cursed is everyone who hangs [crucified] on a tree (cross)"—in order that in Christ Jesus the blessing of Abraham might also come to the Gentiles, so that we would all receive [the realization of] the promise of the [Holy] Spirit through faith.
>
> —GALATIANS 3:13–14

The Lord will rescue me from every evil assault, and He will bring me safely into His heavenly kingdom; to Him be the glory forever and ever. Amen.

—2 TIMOTHY 4:18

It's time to use your own words, the authority of heaven, and the anointing of the Holy Spirit to destroy all satanic dedications and agreements that have bound you through your family's bloodlines, things you have said, or things other people did and said to you when you were too young to understand. Get violent and aggressive on the devil as you pray these prayers aloud.

FIRE PRAYERS

In the name of Jesus, I confess the sins of my ancestors. (Whenever possible, name these sins.)

Lord, in Jesus' name, I ask You to forgive me, my mother, and my father for any demonic dedications made over my life.

Let the blood of Jesus destroy every satanic dedication and agreement that came through religious practices and worldly involvements wrapped in satanic influences. I break and destroy the cords that are wrapped around me. Loose me now, in Jesus' name.

I renounce and uproot any evil dedication placed on my life from the day I was born until this day, in Jesus' name.

By the power of the blood of Jesus Christ, I break and destroy every evil ordination, every demonic ceremony dedication, and every known and unknown legal right—whether it was for me, a family member on either side of my bloodline, or any brother or sister in the body of Christ. I break, destroy, and uproot any evil mystical alignments and every satanic dedication and agreement. Let all of it burn off me by the fire of the Holy Spirit. In Jesus' name, amen.

I give notice to all demons associated with any evil dedications and agreements I once entered: I hereby break every contract and every legal right formerly associated with those dedications and agreements, in the mighty name of Jesus Christ.

Lord, cancel every evil consequence that came through my mother's bloodline and my father's bloodline. Break them completely off me today, in the name of Jesus.

I command every demon associated with anything I have been committed to, anything I have given myself to, and everything my parents or my family dedicated me to, to loose me now, in the name of Jesus Christ.

In the name of Jesus, I destroy every principality and power that is over my life.

I completely and fully destroy all wickedness that is over my life from high places, in the name of Jesus.

I destroy all evil dominion. I bind the strongman. I break poverty and unemployment. I break misery. I break every curse, vex (meaning anything that is demonically plaguing or vexing you), *and all voodoo over my life through demonic and satanic dedications and agreements. In the name of Jesus, amen.*

In Jesus' name, I break off every demon that has been assigned with any satanic dedications. (Call out the names based on the dedications you accepted.) Loose me now. Then go to wherever the Lord Jesus Christ sends you, never to return.

I break every witchcraft dedication over my life, in the name of Jesus.

I destroy any evil assignments and projects I was once involved with, in the name of Jesus.

I break every known and unknown demonic meeting I attended that included demonic influences, demonic strongholds, and satanic agreements (all levels and kinds) and to which I dedicated my time, body, and mind. They include transcendental and other ungodly forms of meditation, any form of yoga, and any wicked mystical practice. I command those devils to loose me now, in the name of Jesus. Let the blood of Jesus close the doors behind me now.

By the blood of Jesus that covers me, I cancel my connection to every demon that vexed or cursed me; that brought frustrations, hindrances, delays, or blockages; that involved me in associations of practices, devotion, or allegiance; that accepted loyalty promised by any family member on my behalf; or that was part of any friendship that invited me or that I accepted, surrendering myself to the dark and demonic forces. They are severed today, in Jesus' name.

I take authority over all demonic dedications and agreements, known and unknown, and I curse them to the root. Let them shrivel up and die, in the name of Jesus.

I take authority over every satanic practice and demonic alignment that entered my life from day one. I curse it to the root. Let it shrivel up and die and be uprooted from my life today. In the mighty name of Jesus.

Today I come into agreement with the Holy Spirit to purify my entire life and baptize it in the blood of Jesus Christ. There will never be any agreements of any kind between me and the devil and his demons. My life belongs to Jesus Christ and Him alone.

Father, I celebrate, honor, and worship You. I praise You for my deliverance, in the unmatchable, all-powerful name of Jesus Christ.

Chapter 11

PRAYERS TO DESTROY THE GATES
OF HELL OVER YOUR LIFE

Jesus told Peter, "Now I say to you that you are Peter (which means 'rock'), and upon this rock I will build my church, and all the powers of hell will not conquer it" (Matt. 16:18, NLT). My brother or sister, if Jesus Christ is your Lord and Savior, take what God told Peter and make it your own because it's also meant for you in this lifetime.

The gates of hell have to do with the agendas, plots, schemes, and wiles that the enemy has planned. He uses them because he wants to take over or destroy what God has started and wants to complete in our lives. We know there are gates and portals in the spirit realm. We know the enemy wants the legal right to come and go in our lives, as though there were a revolving door for his personal use.

I was caught in that revolving door for twenty-five years. I remember a very cold day in the South Bronx when a bad feeling followed me. As it did, I had a recurring thought about going to my aunt's house, so I went and rang her bell. I found her and two other people in a witchcraft reading. That was nothing new to me, but one of the people, a man, got my attention. I had never sensed the kind of power he carried. Before my visit was over, he prophesied over me, and I got a major promotion in the satanic realm. From the moment I saw him, I wanted what he had. But getting it meant the devil's revolving door would spin only faster in my life.

In the name of Jesus, it is time to possess the gates of hell and prevent them from prevailing so the plan God has designed for you is not altered in any way, shape, or form. The gates of hell *will not* prevail against it. You need to be on not only the defense but also the offense. That is where you conquer the hosts of hell. When they try to attack you, they will fail miserably and never rise up against you or anything God has given you ever again.

Using the following fire prayers, you are going to attack the demons, maybe like you never have before. Like a piñata at a party, you will beat down those devils and watch candy come out of their pockets. It is time to put them in their place. No devil will be allowed to possess anything God has given you. You are going to destroy those operations and conquer the gates (the agendas) of hell. But first, declare this scripture over your life:

> Blessing I [the LORD] will bless you, and multiplying I will multiply your descendants as the stars of the heaven and as the sand which is on the seashore; and your descendants shall possess the gate of their enemies.
>
> —GENESIS 22:17, NKJV

It's time to lock and load with prayer.

FIRE PRAYERS

Father, You have blessed the seed of Abraham to possess the gates of his enemies. Let that be my story, in the name of Jesus.

I release the fire of the Holy Spirit and the blood of Jesus to destroy all my enemies today, in Jesus' name.

Let any gate of the devil against my life, family, marriage, child(ren), ministry, purpose, and destiny be destroyed by the fire of God today. In Jesus' name, amen.

Let every evil gate that is blocking my blessings, purpose, and destiny be destroyed and uprooted today, in Jesus' name.

I release the fire of heaven to destroy every demonic doorkeeper of the gates of hell that has plotted against me. Let them be destroyed, in Jesus' name.

I cage up every demon that is plotting against me in any way, in Jesus' name.

I destroy the gates of hell. Let every agenda that has my name on it and every plot and scheme be destroyed, removed, uprooted, cursed to the root, and shriveled up. Let them die, in Jesus' name.

I release fire from heaven on every gate or portal, every open door, and every demon that has made its way into my purpose and destiny. Just as Pharaoh drowned in the Red Sea (Exod. 14:26–28), let them drown in the blood of Jesus now.

Right now, I destroy in the blood of Jesus every demon and demonic transaction that the devil has plotted against me.

I release my family, myself, and my ministry, purpose, destiny, and finances from the gates of hell. They will not prevail. Let them be burned to ashes, in Jesus' name.

I destroy every demonic agenda, every satanic monitoring device that surveils me, my family, my church, and my ministry in the spirit realm. Let their eyes be plucked out, and let them be blinded forever, in Jesus' name.

I renounce Satan and his hosts of hell, known and unknown, that are trying to destroy my purpose and my destiny. Let them drown in the blood of Jesus, completely and fully. In Jesus' name, amen.

I release the anointing and authority God has given me to destroy the gates of hell—every evil work, plot, and scheme from the north, south, east, and west. Let them drown in the blood of Jesus.

Let the fire of God destroy any altars that have my name on them and every entrapment that has been set against me and my family, church, ministry, purpose, destiny, finances, marriage, and child(ren). We will rise up; we will live and not die and will declare the works of the Lord (Ps. 118:17). Together we will pulverize the gates of hell, once and for all. In Jesus' untouchable and mighty name, amen.

Chapter 12

PRAYERS THAT DEMOLISH SATANIC MONITORING SYSTEMS

THE APOSTLE PAUL made spiritual warfare very plain. We need to take to heart what he wrote under the Holy Spirit's inspiration: "Our struggle is not against flesh and blood [contending only with physical opponents], but against the rulers, against the powers, against the world forces of this [present] darkness, against the spiritual forces of wickedness in the heavenly (supernatural) places" (Eph. 6:12).

I think we as believers and the church at large have become divided over the issue of spiritual warfare. Because we are not in agreement, we are more vulnerable to the enemy. The devil monitors everything we are taught, everything we do, and everything we say. His monitoring systems include satanic blueprints against us, and he knows when and how to attack. Like Pharaoh against the Israelites, Satan knows when to release his spiritual chariots.

Satan's blueprint was working in my life long before I came to Christ. The revolving-door story I told you in chapter 11 is a perfect example. A recurring thought nudged me three times. I finally surrendered to it and went to my aunt's house. That set into motion a whole chain of events. Two weeks later I was initiated as a high priest (a rare event in satanic quarters), and the mark of the beast was carved into my flesh. None of this was random. I was drawn into my aunt's witchcraft reading for Satan's own reasons. You could say his spiritual chariots escorted me there. He was fulfilling *his* blueprint for my life.

Satanic monitoring systems are demons that have been assigned to monitor your season, your walk, your prayer life, your devotions, and your dedication to the Lord Jesus Christ. They weaken you and infiltrate your spiritual space so they can set up struggles, strongholds, and bondages in your life. Satan's monitoring systems never quit. You and I need to turn the table on them, in the name of Jesus. God has called us to be His great army, but we need the intelligence that comes from monitoring our enemy. The Holy Spirit has all that intelligence; He knows everything the enemy is doing. But are we paying attention?

Let's wake up, smell the coffee, and open our spiritual eyes. We cannot afford to be clueless about the demonic devices and systems the enemy has arrayed against us in the spirit realm. Demonic agents have been assigned in every believer's spiritual space and atmosphere. They have contaminated our spiritual walks. The devil is wreaking havoc in our lives while we walk around without a spiritual care or concern about what he is doing. We can be equally unaware of God's presence in the battle, as Elisha's servant was:

> The servant of the man of God got up early and went out, and behold, there was an army with horses and chariots encircling the city. Elisha's servant said to him, "Oh no, my master! What are we to do?" Elisha answered, "Do not be afraid, for those who are with us are more than those who are with them." Then Elisha prayed and said, "LORD, please, open his eyes that he may see." And the LORD opened the servant's eyes and he saw; and behold, the mountain was full of horses and chariots of fire surrounding Elisha.
>
> —2 KINGS 6:15–17

Let your eyes be opened like the servant's eyes were so you can see the arsenals of heaven and God's chariots of fire. Use the following fire prayers to wreak havoc against the powers of darkness and gain the victory over every evil, demonic, and satanic monitoring system. Drive the devil's kingdom and all his demons out of your life, once and for all. Pray so that every satanic monitoring agent will suffer great destruction and have their spiritual eyes plucked out. Pray for God to make you stealthy in spiritual battle so you can gain the total victory. Pray these things in the mighty name of Jesus Christ, the captain of heaven's armies, today and forevermore.

FIRE PRAYERS

Father, I thank You that through Your Holy Spirit, You have given me the anointing and fire power I need against the devil and every monitoring system in his kingdom, in Jesus' name.

In the name of Jesus Christ, I release the fire of the Holy Spirit on every demonic monitoring system and all forces of darkness that speak my name. I bring them down, completely and fully. Let them be destroyed today by the blood of Jesus.

I pick up the sword and run into battle the way David ran toward Goliath. I destroy and chop down every evil monitoring device that continually watches me, my family, and my marriage, child(ren), loved ones, ministry, church, purpose, and destiny. I shred it into pieces, in Jesus' name.

Let every evil spirit—every witch, warlock, wizard, and sorcerer—that has been paid to monitor my life through witchcraft and the occult have its spiritual eyes plucked out now, in the name of Jesus.

I destroy and curse to the root every demonic frequency that the devil is using to monitor my life, family, church, purpose, and destiny. I put it in the fire of the Holy Spirit and burn it to ashes, in Jesus' name.

Let every demon and devil that is stalking me in the spirit die now and be drowned in the blood of Jesus, just as Pharaoh and his army were drowned in the Red Sea. In Jesus' name, amen.

Let blindness come on every monitoring spirit now, in Jesus' name.

Let every devil, demon, and territorial principality that has been assigned to monitor me die today, in Jesus' name.

I destroy every satanic dispatching system and every evil unleashed against my days and nights. I break all monitoring and demonic assignments and every evil frequency operating against me. Let them fall to the ground, shrivel up, and die. In Jesus' name, amen.

In the name of Jesus, I put the fire of God on the head of every demon that is trying to track me down in the spirit.

I destroy all demonic evil guards that are trying to surround me and watch every spiritual step I take. Let the sword of the Spirit be plunged into their hearts. In Jesus' name, I pray.

Let all contamination that has fallen on me from every monitoring system be destroyed and removed today, in the name of Jesus.

Let every trick that has my name on it in any demonic or satanic playbook be destroyed by the blood of Jesus Christ.

Let blindness come on every demon, devil, and demonic force that attempts to destroy my purpose and destiny. In the untouchable, unmatchable name of Jesus Christ, amen.

For myself and my family, loved ones, ministry, finances, purpose, and destiny, I plead by the blood of Jesus that all satanic systems mentioning our names in the demonic world, realm, and atmosphere be destroyed, never to rise again. In the mighty name of my Lord and Savior, Jesus Christ, amen.

I praise the name of Jesus, and I thank Him for all the victory that He is giving me today. Amen.

Chapter 13

PRAYERS THAT DESTROY DEMONIC
AND SATANIC ALTARS

To ACCOMPLISH THEIR despicable goals, witches, warlocks, sorcerers, wizards, root workers, and voodoo demonic agents use satanic altars. They dedicate these altars to demonic principalities, territorial spirits, familial spirits, spirits of destruction and premature death, and tormenting spirits of anxiety, oppression, depression, and even suicide. These altars exist to devastate human beings, especially those in the body of Christ.

My precious brother or sister, I know this firsthand because I lived and practiced it. I was dedicated to satanic altars, and I used them to steal, kill, and destroy anyone the devil touched or named for his wicked purposes. Altars work through animal sacrifices and demonic ingredients. I used them to release the hosts and chariots of hell on people. The goal was to completely crush them. At every possible level, I and others put on them spirits of violence, anger, sickness, rebellion, and destruction. We used the spirits of suicide, oppression, and depression to torment them to the point of no return.

Yes, I was a vessel in the devil's kingdom and hierarchy called to release this kind of torment. Satanic altars are operating in every state, city, and country on the planet. Some altars have your name or your loved ones' names on them. If you are winning souls and setting captives free, your ministry's name is on them. The kingdom of darkness uses altars against every person who threatens the devil by engaging in spiritual warfare and deliverance. You can bet your bottom dollar that the devil has your name on some altars, somewhere.

But I have good news: the devil's plots, schemes, and wiles don't have to take you down or prevent your purpose or destiny. You and I are going to fight violently against them and destroy them. Just as our precious Old Testament brothers and sisters brought down the high places, we're going to raise the banner of Jesus Christ over those places and over our lives *today*.

Before you pray the fire prayers, I want you to recite Psalm 91 over your life:

> He who dwells in the shelter of the Most High will remain secure and rest in the shadow of the Almighty [whose power no enemy can withstand]. I will say of the LORD, "He is my refuge and my fortress, my God, in whom I trust [with great confidence, and on whom I rely]!" For He will save you from the trap of the fowler, and from the deadly pestilence. He will cover you and completely protect you with His pinions, and under His wings you will find refuge; His faithfulness is a shield and a wall.
>
> You will not be afraid of the terror of night, nor of the arrow that flies by day, nor of the pestilence that stalks in darkness, nor of the destruction (sudden death) that lays waste at noon. A thousand may fall at your side and ten thousand at your right hand, but danger will not come near you. You will only [be a spectator as you] look on with your eyes and witness the [divine] repayment of the wicked [as you watch safely from the shelter of the Most High]. Because you have made the LORD, [who is] my refuge, even the Most High, your dwelling place, no evil will befall you, nor will any plague come near your tent.
>
> For He will command His angels in regard to you, to protect and defend and guard you in all your ways [of obedience and service]. They will lift you up in their hands, so that you do not [even] strike your foot against a stone. You will tread upon the lion and cobra; the young lion and the serpent you will trample underfoot.
>
> "Because he set his love on Me, therefore I will save him; I will set him [securely] on high, because he knows My name [he confidently trusts and relies on Me, knowing I will never abandon him, no, never]. He will call upon Me, and I will answer him; I will be with him in trouble; I will rescue him and honor him. With a long life I will satisfy him and I will let him see My salvation."
>
> —PSALM 91:1–16

FIRE PRAYERS

Today I serve an eviction notice on every demonic, evil, satanic altar with my name or my family's name engraved on it. Our names are removed now, in the name of Jesus.

I curse to its root every satanic altar that has my birth certificate on it, and I wash it away with the blood of Jesus.

I put the fire of God on every satanic altar designed to steal, kill, and destroy me, my family, or my purpose and destiny (John 10:10). Burn to ashes and be destroyed, in Jesus' name.

Let every demonic altar that is aimed at my finances to bring the spirit of poverty shrivel up and die, in the name of Jesus.

By the blood of Jesus, I break, destroy, and completely pulverize every satanic altar that has anything to do with my name or any spirit of sickness. Let it shrivel up and die, in Jesus' name.

I destroy every satanic altar that has incarcerated my ministry, purpose, or destiny. I curse it to the root. Let it shrivel up and die. Release me now, in Jesus' name. Amen.

Today, I pluck out the eyes of every demonic altar that has monitored me in the spirit realm. Be blinded forever, never to find me again. In Jesus' name, amen.

I destroy every satanic altar right now and remove my name and my family's bloodlines, completely and fully, in Jesus' name.

I say to every demonic altar with spirit husbands, wife spirits, marine spirits, water spirits, accident spirits, divorce devils, and premature death devils: shrivel up and die now. In Jesus' name, amen.

Let the fire of God fall on every satanic altar on which my name has been called into the dark places. Let it be burned and destroyed completely, in Jesus' name.

I break and destroy every demonic altar that has my marriage on it.

It is not my purpose or destiny to live on any satanic altar. Let my purpose and destiny be loosed now, in Jesus' name.

The bloodlines of my children, my children's children, and all my family will be purified and removed from any kind of satanic altar, in Jesus' name.

I cancel every agreement I have made (both known and unknown) that put my name on any satanic altars. Let these agreements and the altars be destroyed today, in Jesus' name.

Let every area of my life be completely and fully delivered, in the mighty name of Jesus Christ.

In Jesus' name, I refuse to come into agreement with the devil and any kind of satanic altar during my dreams.

I cancel any and every agreement that came out of my mouth, heart, or thinking and put my name on any altar. Let those agreements be canceled and destroyed now, in Jesus' name.

Lord Jesus, I walk toward Your cross, leaving behind every evil plot, scheme, wile, association, compromise, and demonic door. I renounce any agreements I have made with any devils, either consciously or unconsciously, that have put (or that I have allowed to put) my name on any satanic altar. I cancel them today and renounce them fully, in the mighty name of Jesus Christ.

Lord God, I give You all the glory and praise. I worship You! Thank You for setting me free, in Jesus' name.

Now end by reciting Psalm 27 over your life, family, and loved ones:

The LORD is my light and my salvation—whom shall I fear? The LORD is the refuge and fortress of my life—whom shall I dread? When the wicked came against me to eat up my flesh, my adversaries and my enemies, they stumbled and fell. Though an army encamp against me, my heart will not fear; though war arise against me, even in this I am confident.

One thing I have asked of the LORD, and that I will seek: that I may dwell in the house of the LORD [in His presence] all the days of my life, to gaze upon the beauty [the delightful loveliness and majestic grandeur] of the LORD and to meditate in His temple. For in the day of trouble He will hide me in His shelter; in the secret place of His tent He will hide me; He will lift me up on a rock. And now my head will be lifted up above my enemies around me, in His tent I will offer sacrifices with shouts of joy; I will sing, yes, I will sing praises to the LORD.

Hear, O LORD, when I cry aloud; be gracious and compassionate to me and answer me. When You said, 'Seek My face [in prayer, require My presence as your greatest need],' my heart said to You, 'Your face, O LORD, I will seek [on the authority of Your word].' Do not hide Your face from me, do not turn Your servant away in anger; You have been my help; do not abandon me nor leave me, O God of my salvation! Although my father and my mother have abandoned me, yet the LORD will take me up [adopt me as His child].

Teach me Your way, O Lord, and lead me on a level path because of my enemies [who lie in wait]. Do not give me up to the will of my adversaries, for false witnesses have come against me; they breathe out violence. I would have despaired had I not believed that I would see the goodness of the LORD in the land of the living. Wait for and confidently expect the LORD; be strong and let your heart take courage; yes, wait for and confidently expect the LORD.

Chapter 14

PRAYERS AGAINST SPIRITUAL WITCHCRAFT MANIPULATION

MANIPULATION INVOLVES WITCHCRAFT, occult, and demonic powers that are used to influence, dominate, and ultimately destroy people. Before Christ took me to hell in October 1999, I lived as a master of witchcraft manipulation and held a spiritual PhD in the subject. I operated in the shadows of the demonic in the devil's kingdom, which is the highest hierarchy of the satanic realm. I did it to infiltrate the church and conduct demonic spiritual warfare against the church and the world.

The awesomeness of God cannot be talked about; it has to be displayed. The majesty of His holiness was displayed over my life in 1999. The only reason the story is incredible is that God's fingerprint is on it. I never knew anything about the Bible or about the man called the apostle Paul. But when I read the life of Paul, I found to my amazement that my life was very parallel to his.

We know from the Book of Acts that Paul was recruited by Jesus Christ Himself, who asked him, "Why are you persecuting Me?" That's when Paul answered, "Who are You, Lord?" (See Acts 9:4–5.) I believe that Jesus called to him from the third heaven, where God sits and where Paul was caught up and saw a vision (2 Cor. 12:1–6).

That is deep and profound. When I read it, it moved my heart deeply. When I was seven and a half years old, I was recruited from the second heaven, where principalities and the devil himself moved from his kingdom. I told you about the necklace that fell at my feet from the second heaven and represented the seven demonic powers of the dark side. That necklace ushered me into twenty-five years of life in the despicable satanic kingdom. That necklace stole my childhood.

But the same Jesus Christ who recruited the great apostle Paul had a plan and a purpose for me. At thirty-five years old, my journey from darkness to light started, and my life has never been the same. In all the years since that night in 1999, my Lord and Savior Jesus Christ has lavished

His goodness, mercy, and grace on me. Nothing about my twenty-five years with the devil could ever compare in any way. Today, I feel like the donkey that was tied up somewhere in bondage but got to carry Jesus into Jerusalem (Mark 11:1–11). As He did with that donkey, Jesus knew my condition and my address, and He sent the Holy Spirit for me. I praise Him and thank Him every day of my life for rescuing me. To God be the glory, in Jesus' name.

THE DAMAGES OF A MANIPULATION SPIRIT

In my "B.C." years (before knowing Christ), I understood, practiced, and used witchcraft manipulation to conquer, destroy, and control all kinds of people. It is like sinking your claws into people who are under anesthesia. They don't realize that something diabolical is controlling them, and they can't release themselves.

A story in Mark's Gospel shows what manipulation does to human beings:

> They came to the other side of the sea, to the region of the Gerasenes. When Jesus got out of the boat, immediately a man from the tombs with an unclean spirit met Him, and the man lived in the tombs, and no one could bind him anymore, not even with chains. For he had often been bound with shackles [for the feet] and with chains, and he tore apart the chains and broke the shackles into pieces, and no one was strong enough to subdue and tame him. Night and day he was constantly screaming and shrieking among the tombs and on the mountains, and cutting himself with [sharp] stones. Seeing Jesus from a distance, he ran up and bowed down before Him [in homage]; and screaming with a loud voice, he said, "What business do we have in common with each other, Jesus, Son of the Most High God? I implore you by God [swear to me], do not torment me!" For Jesus had been saying to him, "Come out of the man, you unclean spirit!" He was asking him, "What is your name?" And he replied, "My name is Legion; for we are many." And he began begging Him repeatedly not to send them out of the region.
>
> —MARK 5:1–10

Demons had this man so bound that when Jesus asked him his name, they spoke for him. Darkness and territorial demonic forces entrenched themselves in him and controlled him from head to toe, day and night. He could not think his own thoughts or answer Jesus with his own words.

When I was ten years old, demons had already spoken for me. My spiritual godmothers taught me how to thank the gods that received me into the satanic kingdom. After several days, when certain rituals were completed, those godmothers sent me back to my mother. But I was not the same boy. I was still a child, but my innocence was gone. I no longer belonged to my mother; other entities owned me. Now, guardian spirits controlled me, and I attended weekly training sessions, where I learned diabolical things. A dark system swallowed me whole and kept me there for decades.

Many people are bound by similar witchcraft systems today. Not all of them become Satan's official workers, as I did. Yet they can't decide, talk, or think for themselves. They are like spiritual zombies, held directly or indirectly by devils called *manipulation*. These devils have manipulated not only our marriages, children, and society but also the church. Paul warned the church at Galatia about this:

> The practices of the sinful nature are clearly evident: they are sexual immorality, impurity, sensuality (total irresponsibility, lack of self-control), idolatry, sorcery, hostility, strife, jealousy, fits of anger, disputes, dissensions, factions [that promote heresies], envy, drunkenness, riotous behavior, and other things like these. I warn you beforehand, just as I did previously, that those who practice such things will not inherit the kingdom of God.
>
> —GALATIANS 5:19–21

If ever we needed the Holy Spirit, we need Him now to destroy all witchcraft spirits and break their attempts on, in, and through us. Our families and loved ones, as well as our homes, ministries, purposes, and destinies need to be freed from the spirit of manipulation, which is also known as the spirit of Jezebel.

By the power of the Holy Spirit, the fire prayers you are about to pray are able to destroy all types of manipulation over your life. Whatever season you are in, it is time to fast and pray and trust the Lord Jesus

Christ to destroy, dismantle, and uproot all chaos and every manipulating spirit that is over your mind, heart, soul, family, home, and marriage. It is time to release the spirit of Elijah on these devils, call fire from heaven, and let it fall on their heads.

Are you ready to receive your victory from the Holy Spirit? We're going to release the arsenals of God on every wicked spirit that has gripped, incarcerated, and manipulated you on any spiritual level, whether you knowingly or unknowingly allowed it. But before you pray these prayers, confess before God any sin that is in your life and ask Him to forgive and cover you in the blood of Jesus Christ. Ask the Holy Spirit to give you a fresh anointing to destroy any works of darkness over your life, in the mighty name of Jesus Christ.

FIRE PRAYERS

Let the thunder and the lightning bolts of God get and destroy every demonic target in the enemy's camp that has my name on it. (Psalm 18:13 says, "The LORD also thundered in the heavens, and the Most High uttered His voice, {amid} hailstones and coals of fire.") *Let every spirit of witchcraft and manipulation be brought down and burned to ashes, in Jesus' name.*

Let every mind-controlling devil that has directed my thinking be destroyed today, along with every demonic force that has wrapped itself around any part of my life, in Jesus' name.

Today, I put the fire and judgment of God on any altars of witchcraft against my family, name, purpose, and identity. Let those altars burn to ashes. In Jesus' name, amen.

Let every witch, warlock, and sorcerer that has sent witchcraft and the manipulation spirit against any aspect of my life, family, ministry, or church be completely and fully destroyed, in Jesus' name.

I put the fire of God on every hiding place in the demonic realm of the spirit. Let it burn out any devils that have tracked, stalked, and manipulated me, and let them drown in the blood of Jesus. In Jesus' name, amen.

I release the consuming fire of the Holy Spirit on every devil and witch that has infiltrated my home, church, or business. Today, they will shrivel up and die. In Jesus' name, amen.

I destroy every satanic altar of manipulation devils, witchcraft devils, and mind-control devils. I burn to ashes all altars and demonic assignments against my life. In Jesus' name, amen.

I pull down any veil of darkness that is over my mind, along with all cloudiness and satanic darkness that covers my heart, controls my thinking, or manipulates me in any way. Let them be destroyed now, in Jesus' name.

By the blood of Jesus, I destroy every known and unknown witchcraft curse that is working against me.

I destroy any demonic covenants or demonic vows I have made with the devil and his demons through manipulation over my life. In the name of Jesus, let them be destroyed.

By the fire of God, I destroy every demonic arsenal of witchcraft that is set against me. In Jesus' name, I pray. Amen.

In Jesus' name, I break, destroy, and dismantle every witchcraft devil, manipulation devil, and demonic assignment of the enemy against me and my family.

In Jesus' name, let every entrapment of witches and warlocks that has been chasing me, whether in my sleep or my waking hours, be destroyed.

I completely and fully destroy every plot, scheme, and wile of the devil against me, my family, my church, and my ministry. Let these evil means drown now in the blood of Jesus.

In Jesus' name, I break and destroy all forms of witchcraft and every bewitchment that is over my life.

Holy Spirit, deliver my mind today, in the name of Jesus.

Holy Spirit, deliver my finances today. In Jesus' name, I break all forms of witchcraft against my finances.

I break every curse of poverty over my finances, life, family, and home, in Jesus' name.

In the name of Jesus, I break every witchcraft demon over my health. Let it burn, shrivel up, and die.

In Jesus' name, I destroy every council of witches and warlocks that has released manipulation spirits against me.

In the name of Jesus, I send the fire of God on the devil's camp and against any witches invoking my name.

(Lay your right hand on the top of your head and say the following.) *I kill in the spirit realm all damages to my purpose and destiny that were caused by witches, warlocks, spiritual assignments against my life, and manipulation devils. By the blood of Jesus, I destroy those devils today. Lord, release me now, in Jesus' name.*

I destroy every demonic manipulation spirit that is holding back my spiritual inheritance. Let that manipulation burn to ashes, in Jesus' name.

I destroy every warlock, witch, and demonic spirit that has crept into my dreams to manipulate and control my purpose and my destiny. Let these evil workers be destroyed, in Jesus' name.

I command the fire of the Holy Spirit to purify and sanctify me. Holy Spirit, fill up every void in my mind, heart, spirit, and soul. In Jesus' name, amen.

In Jesus' name, I release the anointing of the Holy Spirit on, in, and through me.

In the name of Jesus, I release the oil of heaven to fill and overflow my cup with the anointing of the Holy Spirit over my life.

Lord, I stand in agreement with the Holy Spirit's renewing of my life, from the crown of my head to the soles of my feet. In Jesus' name, amen.

Chapter 15

PRAYERS TO DESTROY SATANIC ASTRAL-PROJECTING ATTACKS

L ET ME DESCRIBE to you what astral-projecting is, as many people have different concepts and ideas about it. Many witches and warlocks use astral-projecting to come to your home and curse your marriage and children. Others project themselves into your home to stir fear and terror. And some first shift themselves into animals before terrorizing you.

In astral-projecting the spirit of the person separates from the material body so the person can travel outside the body in the spirit realm. This out-of-body experience is possible through demonic influences and a demonic contract or covenant called the silver cord. It's not an actual cord but refers to the contract made to astral-project. When your prayers destroy the silver cord, the person cannot astral-project into your home or business to curse you. There is a possibility, through no fault of yours, that when you break that contract, the person who was astral-projecting will not return to his or her body and can be pronounced dead.

I remember all this like it was yesterday. I had an upper-level contract with one of the highest-ranking demonic forces to leave my body (astral-project) to curse neighborhoods, communities, and even regions. If a spirit of poverty existed, I could curse the area and bind the atmosphere so the poverty would continue. I could do the same to keep people in bondage to homosexuality, alcohol, sickness, and drugs.

Today, I'm going to teach you how to break those strongholds and bondages through prayer. We are commanded to pray for the nations and for our neighbors, communities, homes, and brothers and sisters everywhere who might be tormented by demonic forces, witches, and warlocks. In my travels and in the many emails I receive, I learn of people who are suffering this way. Some are fighting the good fight against people who are astral-projecting into their homes.

I have bad news for everyone who is operating in the demonic. But I have good news for you. People have astral-projected into your home for the last time. By the power of the Holy Spirit, you are going to take care of that issue, once and for all.

FIRE PRAYERS

In the name of Jesus, I declare that the heavens will hear my voice as I break down, destroy, and dismantle every demonic atmosphere (Deut. 32:1; Ps. 138:1).

Holy Spirit, release the judgment of God on every astral-projection silver cord today. Let it be destroyed, dismantled, and uprooted. In Jesus' name, amen.

In the name of Jesus, let every demonic warlock and witch of darkness that is astral-projecting against me be brought down to the ground, right now. Let the silver cord be destroyed, never to arise again. In Jesus' name.

In the name of Jesus, I put the fire of God on every astral-projecting demon that is trying to infiltrate my home and dreams. Let it be destroyed now.

I destroy every kind of satanic contract, demonic covenant, and silver cord that enables astral-projecting into my home; I curse it to the root. Let it shrivel up and die. In Jesus' name, amen.

By the fire of the Holy Spirit, let every devil that is astral-projecting to carry out demonic assignments against my life, family, ministry, and business burn to the ground. In Jesus' name, amen.

May the angels of the Lord encamp around me and my family, home, purpose, and destiny (Ps. 34:7). In the mighty name of Jesus Christ, amen.

Today, in the name of Jesus, I take over the atmospheres and airways of every astral-projecting devil, and I confuse them in the air. Let the silver cord now be destroyed completely, in the name of Jesus.

In the name of Jesus, I uproot every demonic silver cord of astral-projecting. I separate the person and the demon, and I void the demonic assignment now, in Jesus' name.

With every demonic person who is traveling in the spirit realm to spy on me, I destroy the contract between you and the demon. Let it be known in the demon world that you will no longer be able to operate at any level of the satanic kingdom to astral-project ever again, in Jesus' name.

In the name of Jesus, I strip naked every demonic warlock, witch, and sorcerer that is trying to come against me.

Let the judgment of God fall on the head of every devil that is trying to torment me, my family, and my loved ones by astral-projecting. Let them be tormented night and day until they come to repentance. In Jesus' name, I pray.

Let every witch that is astral-projecting into my church, ministry, home, or business to void, alter, or edit my purpose and destiny be prevented as I put the fire of God on every silver cord. Let each contract burn to ashes, in the name of Jesus.

By the fire of the Holy Spirit, I completely and fully destroy every satanic council. In Jesus' name, amen.

Father God, bring Your judgment on every astral-projecting witch and warlock, and let the silver cord be destroyed now, in the name of Jesus.

Let the fire of the Holy Spirit take vengeance on every astral-projecting satanic agent. I destroy your assignment over every region, state, and community. I destroy your evil plan and evil work by the fire of the Holy Spirit. Be brought down to nothing, in Jesus' name.

Father, I thank You that my enemy has been disgraced and that all assignments of astral-projecting against my church, family, ministry, home, marriage, purpose, and destiny have been canceled by the blood of Jesus Christ. I claim the victory over them today and forevermore, in Jesus' mighty name. Amen.

Lord Jesus Christ, I praise You and thank You for the victory!

Chapter 16

PRAYERS TO DESTROY SATANIC HINDRANCES AND DELAYS

T HE DEVIL SHOOTS fiery arrows at his targets (Eph. 6:16). They are
called *hindrance, delay, blockage,* and *distraction.* They are designed
to frustrate your purpose, your destiny, your current season, and the
season you are about to enter. If you are a believer who is following Jesus
Christ, the kingdom of darkness uses these strategies to discourage you
and eventually separate you from God's will.

It's sad to say that these strategies are very effective, and many beautiful brothers and sisters in Christ have struggled because of them. I have
experienced hindrance and delay in areas of my life. Sometimes it feels
as if I have taken two steps forward and been shoved four steps back. In
altar calls, I've seen believers crying their hearts out because they haven't
seen a breakthrough or any sign of advancing. Many live in discouragement and disappointment, and some even question God.

That is not God's will for your life, but this is: "Little children
(believers, dear ones), you are of God and you belong to Him and have
[already] overcome them [the agents of the antichrist]; because He who
is in you is greater than he (Satan) who is in the world [of sinful man-
kind]" (1 John 4:4).

REJECT THE COPYCATS

Hindrance and delay cause pain. Through manipulation, these two devils
walk together to entrap you and stifle your walk with God. Their plan is
to wear you down so you stop pursuing the good things God has for you.
Demons are committed to their mission. They try to put you on a path
that looks like God's path but is a copycat, a fake. Unless you have great
discernment and a deep relationship with the Holy Spirit, you can end
up walking in the Spirit but on the wrong road. As Proverbs 14:12 says,
"There is a way which seems right to a man and appears straight before
him, but its end is the way of death."

It's not only new believers who fall for copycat paths. It happens to mature believers too. It can happen when somebody prophesies that you are going to be a great evangelist or pastor or missionary. If you run with the prophecy instead of taking it to the Lord in prayer, you can find yourself on a journey to nowhere. Your pathway will be full of hindrance, delay, blockage, distraction, and discouragement—everything the devil wants to accomplish.

I can remember when I was a young believer and many brothers told me, "You're going to be a great evangelist for Jesus Christ one day."

I nodded and smiled. Then I took their words to prayer and asked the Lord, "What do You say I'm going to be?"

Sometime later the Lord gave me an amazing dream about being in the house of the great evangelist Nicky Cruz. In the dream, Nicky gave me a giant white box that glowed with the anointing. Then Nicky said, "Hey, John, these are all my sermons. I want you to have them."

I answered, "Nicky, it's impossible for me to take them. You have worked so hard to speak for God and to have that anointing of the Holy Spirit to preach those sermons to the world."

He replied, "No, John, I want you to have them."

I answered, "OK, Nicky. Thank you so much for blessing me with this incredible opportunity."

Then I said, "Nicky, I'm going to step into your kitchen and get a glass of water."

As I approached the kitchen, a man stood there. But he didn't look human. He was wearing demonic necklaces, and he had eyes like a demon-possessed person. I looked straight at him and woke up at that moment, saying, "Maybe Nicky gave me his sermons because he is going to the dark side."

The dream baffled me. I remember phoning some precious pastors I knew and telling them about the dream. I asked if they would pray and ask God for the interpretation so I would know what the dream meant. But sometime later they still couldn't interpret the dream. The Holy Spirit was very upset with me and said, "Did you ask them about your calling, or did you ask Me?"

I answered, "Holy Spirit, I asked You."

He replied, "Then why did you ask them about the dream? I can interpret it for you."

In that moment, my heart broke. I repented and said, "Holy Spirit, please forgive me for undermining You. I should have gone to You first."

The devil was trying to set me up for hindrance and delay. Thank God for the Holy Spirit, who interpreted the dream. He told me that in it, Nicky Cruz represented evangelism in the body of Christ, and God was telling me to be an evangelist for the Lord Jesus Christ. The box that Nicky gave me contained all the sermons I would be preaching in my lifetime. The demonic man in the kitchen represented those in the satanic kingdom who are bound and sitting in darkness, including those in the occult or witchcraft and those under every other demonic attack from the pit of hell. God would be using me to set the captives free through spiritual warfare and deliverance. That was the purpose of the dream. Today, I am living that purpose and destiny, in the name of Jesus.

DESTROY THE SATANIC WEAPONS OF THE DEMONIC KINGDOM

Many believers who want to know their purposes and destinies labor in prayer and even fast, with few, if any, results. The devil has arranged to block their progress. Instead of fasting and praying about their destinies, they should be fasting and praying to curse and dismantle the devil's hindrances and delays. They need to move the spiritual rocks out of the way so the spiritual water can flow. Then, in the Lord's timing, His blessings will rain down and His plan will become clear.

Let me add two more points before you pray: First, remember what King David said: "The LORD is my Shepherd" (Ps. 23:1). That statement hits the devil and his loser demons like an atomic bomb. You need to let them and every hindrance and demonic delay know that the Lord is your Shepherd. That means you are fighting them from the third and highest heaven, where you are seated with Jesus Christ. From there every foul, wicked devil of hindrance and delay that has plagued, manipulated, and entrapped you will be brought down like the walls of Jericho.

Second, every hindrance or delay that you have experienced has a name. Let the devil know that you are going to dismantle all of them. You are going to curse them to their roots, and they will shrivel up and die, in Jesus' name.

It's time to pray.

FIRE PRAYERS

Father, I thank You that You are my Shepherd and that Your hand is on my life. I glorify and praise You, in Jesus' name.

Lord, I know that even when I don't sense it, You always hear my prayers (1 Pet. 3:12; 1 John 5:15). I thank You for that, in Jesus' name.

I speak to every door of progress in my life, and I tell it to open now, in Jesus' name.

Lord, I thank You for being the key that opens every door in my life. In Jesus' name, amen.

Today, I stand before this mountain of hindrance, knowing that I have the anointing to overcome every demonic roadblock and obstacle. Therefore, I curse the mountain to the root. Let it shrivel up and die, in Jesus' name.

In the name of Jesus, I remove my name from every satanic altar of hindrance and delay.

I release the fire of the Holy Spirit on every hindrance, delay, blockage, and distraction that came through a door I consciously or unconsciously opened. Let it be destroyed today, in Jesus' name.

I command lightning to strike the head of every satanic hindrance and delay. In the name of Jesus, let the judgment of God fall on their heads and release me now.

By the power of the Holy Spirit, I destroy every hindrance of demonic shame and guilt. I renounce every spirit of rejection and failure and every embarrassment through people, ministries, and pastors that have stopped me from accessing God's best in my life. In Jesus' name, I pray.

In Jesus' name, I destroy every satanic or demonic oppression and depression that has brought hindrance or delay into my life.

In Jesus' name, I put the devils of hindrance and delay on notice to release my mind and my thoughts now.

I break every satanic yoke that has been wrapped around my neck. I destroy it now, in the name of Jesus.

In Jesus' name, I destroy every demonic network that is operating against my purpose and destiny and trying to hinder or delay me from walking in God's perfect will for my life.

In the name of Jesus, I break and destroy every hindrance of sickness and every infirmity devil that comes on my body. Let them drown in the blood of Jesus Christ today.

I destroy every frustration and all anger, bitterness, resentment, and rebellion that has jumped on me as a result of any hindrance or delay. Get off me now, in Jesus' name.

In Jesus' name, I destroy every hindering form of anxiety in my life.

In Jesus' name, I bind and rebuke all demonic reinforcements that are trying to bring satanic hindrance and delay over my life, in my life, and through my life.

I call out every hindrance spirit and spirit of delay. (You know what your involvements are; you know what has stopped you; you know what has delayed or entrapped you. Name it now.) *Lord, I curse it to the root. Let it shrivel up and die, in Jesus' name.*

In Jesus' name, I completely and fully destroy every hindrance or delay that is trying to kill my purpose and destiny.

I destroy every hindrance, delay, and entrapment of the devil that is trying to destroy the anointing over my life. Let every evil strategy be vanquished by the blood of Jesus.

I release the fire of heaven on every demon of delay, in Jesus' name.

In Jesus' name, I ask the Holy Spirit to pour the oil of heaven on my head.

Lord, restore to me seven times what the cankerworm and the locust have stolen from me (Prov. 6:31; Joel 2:25, KJV). Remove every hindrance, delay, and roadblock of the enemy. Let all of them be destroyed by the blood of Jesus.

Lord, I thank You for this victory, and I worship You in spirit and in truth (John 4:24). Lord, I am moving forward because You are with me. And because You are with me, who can be against me? If You have blessed me, who can curse me? (Rom. 8:31; Num. 23:8).

Lord, I give You all praise and glory. I worship You and thank You for the breakthrough and for all Your blessings. Let every void in my life be filled by the Holy Spirit. Let Him purify and sanctify me and give me revelation and clarity.

In the name of Jesus, I believe every devil of hindrance and delay has died. What is left are the greater things God has for me. In the mighty name of Jesus Christ, I pray. Amen.

Chapter 17
PRAYERS THAT DESTROY THE SPIRIT OF FEAR

THE SPIRIT OF fear is rampant in today's world and is paralyzing and destroying people everywhere. Believers and nonbelievers alike are suffering, and the devil is working around the clock via social media, television, and propaganda from news outlets. Fear is incarcerating entire populations. It may be incarcerating you spiritually, tormenting and oppressing you so that you cannot move or function. Some people won't leave their homes because of the crime rate. They are imprisoned by demonic news reports that create false realities. The devil has established a spirit of fear using tools such as COVID-19 and monkeypox, and many are taking the bait.

Fear has plagued humanity ever since the fall. It keeps people from doing everyday things but also causes them to do things they might never have done in the absence of fear. I remember being in a room with sixteen other men who were about to become satanic priests. We had been chosen, and now we were being prepared for the "big day." When the high priest told us there was no turning back, he meant it. Anyone who did not complete the ritual would be branded a coward and would come under a death sentence. One of the sixteen men looked at me in fear and then looked away. I suspect he had second thoughts about what he was getting into. Yet his own fear kept him from walking away.

The devil is a master of fear. But I have bad news for him and good news for us. The good news has no expiration date, and its author is in control. He sits on the throne and laughs at the devil and his cronies, who thought they would have the last laugh. They won't. God's eternal Word says, "You did not receive the spirit of bondage again to fear, but you received the Spirit of adoption by whom we cry out, 'Abba, Father'" (Rom. 8:15, NKJV). Here's more good news: "God has not given us a spirit of fear, but of power and of love and of a sound mind" (2 Tim. 1:7, NKJV).

Stay right where you are, devil, because we're coming to drown the spirit of fear in the blood of Jesus, once and for all. We are on the spiritual offense and will not shrink back, in Jesus' name.

FIRE PRAYERS

By the authority in the name of Jesus Christ, I take a stand against every fear devil and every tormenting devil that is trying to vex me in my mind, heart, spirit, and life. Be destroyed, in Jesus' name. Amen.

In the name of Jesus, I reject every report of fear that is sent my way.

I bind every demonic thought of fear that has incarcerated my mind, paralyzed my heart, and contaminated my thinking. Let it be destroyed completely and fully, in Jesus' name.

Devil, I refuse to move in fear anymore. In the name of Jesus, amen.

I declare over my life, family, purpose, and destiny that no weapon of demonic fear that has been formed against me will accomplish its goal (Isa. 54:17). In Jesus' name, amen.

Let the fire of the Holy Spirit encircle me, my family, and my home. In Jesus' name, let it burn all demonic fearmongering to ashes.

I shut down every demonic plot, scheme, wile, and operation that the devil is using to plant fear in my heart and family. Let all of it be destroyed, in Jesus' name.

I loose myself and my family from any spirit of fear or torment. In Jesus' name, let it be destroyed and uprooted. Let it shrivel and die. In Jesus' name, amen.

I destroy the fear of man and all fears that are trying to incarcerate me. Today is your last day. I now serve you an eviction notice, in the mighty name of Jesus Christ.

Lord, in the name of Jesus, be my shield and the protector over my mind, heart, and soul.

In Jesus' name, I declare over my life, family, ministry, purpose, destiny, work, career, and marriage that God is for me. So who can be against me? (Rom. 8:31).

I cover my heart and mind with the blood of Jesus Christ. In His name, amen.

In Jesus' mighty name, I cover all dreams, all daytime hours and all nighttime hours, in the blood of Jesus Christ, for me and my house.

Devil, listen to me. I refuse to be intimidated by any demonic fear, tactic, plot, or scheme that you bring against me. By the blood of Jesus Christ, I put the judgment of God on your head. In Jesus' name, amen.

Let every enchantment, incantation, and invocation of satanic fear and torment die now, in Jesus' name.

By the blood of Jesus Christ, I destroy every fear of depression, oppression, sickness, and disease that has entered my life through any satanic works of premature death or demonic assignments sent to incarcerate me. I will live and not die. I will declare the works of the Lord for me and my house, ministry, purpose, and destiny (Ps. 118:17). I baptize myself in the blood of Jesus Christ, drowning every hindrance, delay, blockage, and distraction and all fear devils. Just as with Pharaoh, who drowned in the Red Sea, you will never return. I am victorious, and what God has blessed no one can curse (Num. 23:8). In the mighty, untouchable name of Jesus Christ, I pray. Amen.

Almighty God, all glory, honor, and praise are Yours. I thank You and worship You for setting me free, in Jesus' mighty name.

Chapter 18

PRAYERS TO DESTROY DEMONS THAT ATTACK AT NIGHT

HAVING OPERATED FROM a high level of the highest demonic hierarchy, I know how demons function, and I understand the assignments they carry out. They love to torment you by showing up in your home during the night to accomplish those assignments. Nobody gets a pass. Even pastors and leaders are attacked by these night stalkers.

When I was in the demonic world, my assignment was to blueprint people's lives and find the best strategies for attacking them through witchcraft and demonic forces. I did this by sending demons into their homes to choke or incapacitate them. Many felt themselves being grabbed by the throat. They became paralyzed, unable to talk, move, or even scream out the name of Jesus. They could not reach out for help even when their spouses were sleeping beside them. Often demonic forces would torment people through demonic dreams of gunplay, accidents, rape, and illicit sex with people whose faces they could not see. There were many ways to attack people at night.

Once I became a believer, I would dream about the demonic occult people from my life before Christ. In my dreams they would ask me whether I needed a cleansing or another ceremony they could perform. My response was to immediately preach the gospel, which made them visibly angry and frustrated because they could not grab me.

The devil isn't stupid. He always looks for your weakest moment so he can steal, kill, and destroy. If he cannot get you in the daytime, he will come at night. He knows how these overnight fights cause people who have slept a full eight hours to never feel rested. He knows that demonic dreams seem so real that people think they are happening in actual time and space. (I will talk more about demonic dreams in the next two chapters.) We need to destroy these attacks and get our rest so we can be armed and dangerous when morning comes.

The good news is that we are not defenseless. We are Christ's, and

He has equipped us to resist the devil. As you pray the following fire prayers, the weapons of heaven and of the Lord Jesus Christ and the Holy Spirit will bind these devils. They will search out Satan's workers and works and destroy them, once and for all. The door will be permanently closed to their nighttime strategies, and your night season will be blessed, anointed, sanctified, and purified through the Lord Jesus Christ, today and forevermore.

FIRE PRAYERS

Father, in Jesus' name, I dedicate my home to You, from the inside out.

Father, in the mighty name of Jesus, I dedicate to you every family member who lives in this home.

In Jesus' name, I command the arrows dipped in the blood of Jesus to destroy every satanic nighttime attack and the work of every demon that is trying to enter my home and dreams to torment me and my family. Let them be destroyed, in Jesus' name.

In the name of Jesus, I scatter the demonic forces from the north, south, east, and west. I smite them with the blood of Jesus now.

I put the judgment of God on the heads of all evil workers and night stalkers, in Jesus' name.

I destroy every satanic and demonic power of darkness that is trying to creep into my dreams to alter my purpose and destiny. Let them be extinguished today, in Jesus' name.

Now and forever, I reject every nighttime temptation that comes in my dreams, by my bedside, or in my home. Tonight, let everything the devil is trying to put on me and my family drown in the blood of Jesus.

I refuse to come into agreement with any night stalker or satanic force that operates in the night season. As for me and my house, we will serve the Lord Jesus Christ (Josh. 24:15). In Jesus' name, amen.

I put the fire of the Holy Spirit on every demon that has been assigned to destroy me. Burn completely to ashes. In Jesus' name, amen.

I send back to the sender every demonic stalker and night spirit that is operating against me. Let the altar be destroyed, and let the judgment of God fall on their heads so they come to repentance. In Jesus' name, amen.

Father, I release Your wrath on the demons that are standing at my bedside, choking and spiritually paralyzing me so that I cannot even call out the name of Your Son, Jesus Christ. Let those devils be uprooted from my home, completely and fully, never to return. In Jesus' name, I pray. Amen.

Father, I put a wall of fire around my home and family and in every room from the attic to the basement (Zech. 2:5). No devils will enter. In Jesus' name, I cover every doorway and window in His precious blood.

I cover my family, my home, and myself in the blood of Jesus Christ, and I give God the glory, praise, and honor for protecting us, completely and fully. In Jesus' name, amen.

Chapter 19

PRAYERS TO DESTROY SATANIC DREAMS

S ATAN LIKES THE night shift—not only to attack you outright but also to sow demonic seeds into your dreams. He wants you to entertain and cultivate those seeds so they eventually bring his plans to pass in the natural realm. The Bible shows how this works in the story of a farmer whose fields came under enemy attack: "While his men were sleeping, his enemy came and sowed weeds [resembling wheat] among the wheat, and went away. So when the plants sprouted and formed grain, the weeds appeared also" (Matt. 13:25–26).

If the enemy can't sow bad seeds into your mind when you are wide awake, he will try when you are sleeping. He does it through tormenting, demonic dreams that replay in your mind during the day and can wreak havoc in your life. Most people make the mistake of not cursing these dreams to the root. Then, instead of shriveling up and dying, they demand attention and cause worry.

That is exactly what the devil wants. His aim is for you to sleep but not rest. He wants you spiritually tired and vulnerable during the day. Then he can attack you at your weakest moment, spiritually incarcerate and control you, and assert legal rights over your life and your dreams.

I once heard a story about a precious sister who was an RN. An assistant pastor in her church told her, "I had a dream about you. I saw you lying in the street, surrounded by police officers and an ambulance." The devil used that lie to paralyze the woman with tormenting fear to the point that she locked herself in her apartment. Her pastor prayed with her, but she could not shake the torment. She failed to report to work and eventually lost her job. The devil stole her purpose and her destiny—with just the report of a dream.

When I used witchcraft through people's dreams, my number one way to enslave them was to use traumatic scenes. They saw themselves being shot, run over, or involved in some other incident that would cause premature death. I also used animals such as pythons to torment them. Their dreams would be so real that they could not shake them off when they awakened. They would think about their dreams and tell others about them. They entertained and cultivated them, which gave the devil glory. Brooding over those dreams gave the devil legal rights and an opportunity to make them realities.

As soon as I wake up from a despicable demonic dream, I renounce it, curse it to the root, and let it shrivel up and die. I close that spiritual door with the blood of Jesus, and I leave it shut behind me.

You can do the same. It's time to pray and stop these satanic schemes, once and for all.

FIRE PRAYERS

Today, Father, I declare and decree that the blood of Jesus is over my mind and my bed, day and night. In the name of Jesus, amen.

Father, I give You my dreams tonight, and I give You my night. As I lay my head on my pillow, let both be sanctified and purified. In the name of Jesus Christ, amen.

Father, in the name of Jesus, give me good dreams—dreams of my purpose and destiny. As I sleep, give me dreams of my assignment as a believer in You and a vessel of honor. In Jesus' name, amen.

I arrest every demonic assignment and every devil that is using it to infiltrate my dreams. I curse them to the root, today and tonight, in the name of Jesus.

Let every evil and satanic scenario that the devil is trying to deposit in my dreams be burned by the fire of the Holy Spirit, today and tonight, in the name of Jesus.

I destroy all satanic manipulations of my dreams, in the name of Jesus.

I break and destroy every dream of gunshot wounds, demonic harassment, demonic accidents, and premature death that tries to torment me during the night. I curse them now, in Jesus' name, and with His blood I shut the door on them.

I break and loose myself from every curse, vex, voodoo spell, bewitchment, and evil practice that has infiltrated my dreams. I destroy them all, in the name of Jesus.

In Jesus' name, I put fire and judgment on the head of every demon that has planted evil activities and scenes in my dreams to make them a reality in my life. Now let those demons and their plans shrivel up and die.

I break all satanic covenants and break off all witches, war-locks, and sorcerers that are trying to steal my rest or make contracts, agreements, or demonic alignments with me in the satanic world. I crush and rebuke all of them, and I command them to be destroyed by the fire of the Holy Spirit. In Jesus' name, amen.

In the name of Jesus, I curse to the root every demonic doorway, portal, and gateway that the devil has infiltrated in my dreams. I shut those doors with the blood of Jesus Christ. I will have good dreams. I will have rest, and I will have peace and joy in my dreams. In Jesus' name.

Every demonic spiritual animal that has infiltrated my dreams, I cut off your head just as David cut off Goliath's head (1 Sam. 17:51). In Jesus' name, amen.

Father, by the fire of the Holy Spirit, I ask You to purge me, completely and fully. In Jesus' name, amen.

I destroy every evil covenant and intimidation that the devil has put in my dreams to torment me throughout the night. Never again will they infiltrate my dreams. In Jesus' name, amen.

In Jesus name, I destroy every evil the devil brings against me after midnight.

Let all my dreams be covered by the blood of Jesus Christ, from the moment I lay down my head at night to the moment I arise. In Jesus' name, amen.

Father, in the name of Jesus, I release warring angels to stand by my bedside and the bedsides of my loved ones throughout the night.

Holy Spirit, as I lay down my head to sleep, I ask You to anoint me, my family, my purpose, and my destiny, completely and fully. In Jesus' name, amen.

I destroy every spirit of murder and witchcraft and every demonic plot or evil assignment of Satan's kingdom that has crept into my dreams. Let them all be destroyed, in Jesus' name.

Lord, as I arise now, I release myself from any evil dream, and I wash myself in the blood of Jesus, from the crown of my head to the soles of my feet. By the authority and anointing of the Holy Spirit, I send those demonic dreams back to the pit of hell and shut the door on them. In the name of Jesus, amen.

Chapter 20

PRAYERS TO DESTROY SEXUAL DREAMS
OF INCUBUS AND SUCCUBUS

THE DEVIL IS a master of lust and perversion. Today, we see more filth on television, in movies, and in all forms of entertainment than ever before. Premarital sex, adultery, immorality, and perversion have infiltrated our minds through our eyes. Society has so lost its sense of right and wrong that people don't even blush about anything anymore.

I remember when I was a young boy and a friend would ask (in the presence of a young lady), "Hey, you like her?" There was no place to hide, and I would turn as red as a lollipop. Sadly, those "good old" days are gone.

The devil aims to destroy people through infidelity devils, pornography devils, and perversion devils. He gains access through your television, the silver screen, the internet, and the soft pornography in advertisements. On Broadway in New York City, gigantic billboards flash images of women who are practically naked. You cannot escape it. It is right in your face.

That is the strategy the devil and his cronies use. Those images can show up in sexual dreams. You think you are having sex with someone, but it's a demon in disguise. Those experiences create demonic soul ties. If you are married, you can begin to play them out in the physical realm and destroy your family. As a warlock for hire, I put perversion and lust spirits on people's marriages. Their relationships would weaken, one or both partners would commit adultery, and they'd end up in divorce court. Destroying families is the devil's game.

Satan also wants to destroy men. He knows that if he can remove the husband, a family will be crippled. That is key in the current breakdown of the family. So are perversion and lust. In the demonic world I called it the Delilah spirit. It brings men nothing but filth and wickedness, but it masquerades as something desirable. The man is tempted to enjoy it for just a moment, but it leads to destruction—pure and evil.

The devil uses two specific spirits called incubus and succubus. Incubus comes from *incubare,* which means "to lie upon."[1] This demon is a male form that lies upon sleepers, especially women, to have sexual intercourse with them in their dreams. If you don't curse it to its root, the fantasy eventually becomes a reality. It's time to wake up, my sisters, and destroy this thing, especially if you're married.

The succubus demon plays the female counterpart in a man's dreams, to draw him out of his marriage and into fornication. It becomes a spirit husband or spirit wife that performs demonic sexual activities that feel real to the dreamer, even to the point of orgasm. This demon brings hindrances, delays, blockages, and satanic and demonic pregnancies. It also brings abortions, miscarriages, barrenness, and even rape to women. Succubus can result in the molestation of males and females. It brings hell on earth, disaster, and even death.

It's time to destroy and curse this wickedness to its root. Too often we fight the good fight but never conquer anything because we don't deal with the root issue. If we want to be free of these demons, we need to expose and destroy their roots. If you cut down a tree and leave the stump in the ground, it will eventually sprout again. But if you remove the tree and its roots, it will never grow back. In the spiritual realm you have to remove things from the root, completely and fully, so they never return.

We need to feel a holy anger over these devils and release the fire of God to torment them until they shrivel and die forever.

Let's pray.

FIRE PRAYERS

I release the fire and anger of the Lord Jesus Christ on every devil that appears in my dreams at any time.

In the name of Jesus Christ, I curse to the root every demonic sexual perversion demon that has infiltrated my dreams. Let all of them be cut down, in the name of Jesus.

Incubus demon, may the fire of God fall on your head so that you shrivel up and die. In Jesus' name, amen.

Succubus demon, I release the fire of God on your head. Shrivel up and die, in the name of Jesus.

By the sword of the Spirit, I cut down every sexual demon that would try to enter my dreams. In Jesus' name, amen.

I put the judgment of God on every incubus and succubus devil that is trying to come into my dreams to make spiritual marriages and spiritual babies. I release the fire of God to burn you down now, in Jesus' name.

Incubus, be castrated by the fire of the Holy Spirit, in Jesus' name.

Succubus, I command the fire of God to fall on you and your private parts. Be burned to ashes, in the name of Jesus.

In the name of Jesus, I reject all sexual advances of incubus and succubus in my dreams, and I curse all their demonic seductions.

In the name of Jesus, I refuse to give my body to any demon that enters my dreams.

Let every demon of perversion, wickedness, and lust be burned to ashes, in the name of Jesus.

Let every prostitution devil, lust devil, and perversion devil and every door that has been opened to my eye gates, ear gates, and mouth gate be shut down, in the name of Jesus.

Let all satanic lust that has crept into my mind be destroyed by the blood of Jesus Christ.

In the name of Jesus Christ, I baptize all my dreams in His precious blood.

Holy Spirit, awaken me when any sexual demon is trying to creep into my dreams, in Jesus' name.

Let every spirit husband and spirit wife be destroyed by the blood of Jesus now, in Jesus' name.

I destroy and pulverize every demonic marriage certificate completely and fully, by the blood of Jesus Christ.

I reject and curse to the root all demonic marriages, engagement rings, and wedding rings that have been given to me in my dreams by any kind of demon. Let them be destroyed, in Jesus' name.

I curse to the root and will not attend any demonic spiritual weddings in my dreams. Let them be shut down, in Jesus' name.

I rebuke incubus and succubus, and I uproot them from my dreams, once and for all. In Jesus' name, amen.

In Jesus' name, let the fire of God burn out of me any demonic seed that was planted by incubus or succubus.

Let the blood of Jesus wash my body clean, from the crown of my head to the soles of my feet. In Jesus' name, amen.

Let the fire of the Holy Spirit and the oil of heaven fall on my head, from the crown of my head to the soles of my feet. In Jesus' name.

Thank You, Holy Spirit! Lord, I give You glory, honor, and praise, and I thank You for Your victory. In Jesus' name, amen.

Chapter 21

PRAYERS TO DESTROY SATANIC ACCIDENTS AND WITCHCRAFT

THE ONE WHO comes to steal, kill, and destroy has unleashed one of his most demonic soldiers against us. Its goal is to cause collateral damage, grief, pain, and even premature death. He uses this force effectively. It is the spirit of accidents, sent from the pit of hell by Satan himself. I know this firsthand because I served as a demonic hit man. I contracted with demons to unleash car accidents and incidents on the streets that would cause fights and bring harm or death. I dispatched satanic arsenals to destroy marriages through a spirit of death that drove spouses to hurt each other and even grab for knives or guns to kill each other.

Everything I did in my life before Christ is under His blood. I've been forgiven, completely and fully. I share these details not to relive the past but to bring spiritual awareness for you, my brother or sister in Christ. Devils and demonic forces are trying to steal, kill, and destroy your marriage, your loved ones, and *you*.

The devil causes accidents involving vehicles, machinery, and random items. There have been numerous deaths in New York City involving the subway. In one case a homeless man shoved a perfect stranger in front of an oncoming train, killing her.[1] The act was unprovoked, as they often are. I believe this attacker was demon possessed. I suspect that is also true in cases where attackers have struck people with random objects, ending the victims' lives on the spot.

Many incidents that we call "freak accidents" have been orchestrated by the devil. He can arrange for a car to appear suddenly and run you down, when you thought it was safe to cross the street. In 2021 I had a so-called freak accident shortly after a mass deliverance for 180 people around the world. The implanted cataract lens that was in my eye from previous surgeries spontaneously fell out, and I had to have two more operations to fix it. My doctors had never seen anything like it, so they called it a "freak accident." I called it a demonic attack. I praise the Lord

Jesus Christ, who took what the devil meant for evil and turned it around for good.

We will pray specifically against premature deaths in chapter 31. Right now we are focused on deaths from satanic accidents and witchcraft, which can lead to criminal acts. How many times have our hearts broken because someone walked into a school and shot children? I'm pretty sure some of those children were Christians, yet their lives ended prematurely. Let me make this clear: God does not call people to terrible deeds, but the devil cannot do anything unless God allows him. Our part is to fight the good fight of faith. That's how we engage the devil head-on and dismantle every demonic accident, premature death, or satanic attack coming from him and his demonic kingdom. Their mission is to attack. Our mission is to destroy their attacks, in the unmatchable name of Jesus Christ.

I have good news for you: we are going to make that mission plain to these demons by paralyzing them, cursing and uprooting their plans, and causing them to shrivel and die. These demons will not be free to come into your family or attack your loved ones. They cannot feel free to enter a church and shoot up the congregation, either. You are going to pray, as I am. We are going to take back our territory. By the power of the Holy Spirit we will cancel and uproot any demonic accidents, rendering them void, in the mighty name of Jesus Christ. We are going to open our mouths in holy anger and aim our arsenals at the devil's camp, destroying his plans on the spot.

Make sure you don't hold back. Don't be polite or shy. It's time to be aggressive and violent against these demons and their kingdom. (See Matthew 11:12.) They don't stand a chance. In Jesus' name, you are going on the offense to destroy every plot the devil has conjured with your name on it.

FIRE PRAYERS

Father, I thank You for being my shield and protector (Ps. 18:2; 91:4). *In the mighty name of Jesus Christ, amen.*

By the blood of Jesus, I destroy every spirit of accident that comes against me or my spouse, child(ren), home, and extended family, and I put the judgment of God on its head. Let these spirits be tormented day and night, in Jesus' name.

In the blood of Jesus, I baptize my car, bike, motorcycle, and any public transportation that I or my loved ones use.

I call out and I put on notice every spirit of accident at every level. By the blood of Jesus Christ, I crack you over your head, and you will loose me now. Your evil plans will not come to pass. They are canceled, in Jesus' name.

I remove my name and my family members' names from use by any spirit of accident operating in the demonic world. I burn down its altars, in Jesus' name.

I destroy every demonic or satanic spiritual obituary that the devil has written involving my name, family, spouse, child(ren), church, or ministry. I break it completely and fully, in Jesus' name.

I destroy every satanic or demonic funeral that has been prearranged for me or my family members. In the name of Jesus, I curse it to the root now.

I shut down every avenue and demonic highway that has my name or my family members' names on it. I destroy all of them and all premature death now, in the name of Jesus.

In the name of Jesus, I destroy and completely and fully uproot all accidents that have been decreed and spoken over my life.

I cover myself and my family, as well as any journeys that might be targeted for any kind of accident. I destroy all such attempts, in Jesus' name.

Let every witchcraft of accident that has been declared, placed, or attempted over my life be destroyed today, in Jesus' name.

I break and destroy all satanic spells and incantations that have been spoken over my life and my family. In the name of Jesus Christ, let them be completely and fully uprooted.

I dismantle every satanic accident involving planes that I board all the days of my life. Let all such schemes be destroyed, never to be accomplished. In the name of Jesus, amen.

I release the power of God over me and my family to cancel every premature death spirit or accident, in the name of Jesus.

I release warring angels to destroy every demonic assignment, plot, scheme, or wile that would bring accidental death on me or my family. In Jesus' name, amen.

I break and destroy every demonic door, portal, and gateway in the devil's setup that would bring premature death or any demonic accident over myself, my family, my spouse, and my child(ren). I cancel them, in the all-powerful name of Jesus Christ.

Lord Jesus Christ, I cover myself and my family with Your blood, from the tops of our heads to the soles of our feet. No devil or demonic spirit will succeed in bringing pain or grief into our lives through any demonic setup or scheme. I destroy those things, in Jesus' mighty name.

Lord, I give You glory, praise, and worship. Thank You for Your divine protection over me and my family. I rejoice in the words of Isaiah 54:17: "'No weapon that is formed against you will succeed; and every tongue that rises against you in judgment you will condemn. This [peace, righteousness, security, and triumph over opposition] is the heritage of the servants of the LORD, *and this is their vindication from Me,' says the* LORD."

Chapter 22

PRAYERS TO DISMANTLE DEMONS THAT MENTION YOUR NAME

YOUR NAME HAS been mentioned someplace you might not expect: the spirit realm. The Scriptures reveal this in the life of Job, whose name came up in a conversation between God and Satan.

> There was a day when the sons of God (angels) came to present themselves before the LORD, and Satan (adversary, accuser) also came among them to present himself before the LORD. The LORD said to Satan, "From where have you come?" Then Satan answered the LORD, "From roaming around on the earth and from walking around on it." The LORD said to Satan, "Have you considered and reflected on My servant Job? For there is none like him on the earth, a blameless and upright man, one who fears God [with reverence] and abstains from and turns away from evil [because he honors God]. And still he maintains and holds tightly to his integrity, although you incited Me against him to destroy him without cause." Satan answered the LORD, "Skin for skin! Yes, a man will give all he has for his life. But put forth Your hand now, and touch his bone and his flesh [and severely afflict him]; and he will curse You to Your face." So the LORD said to Satan, "Behold, he is in your hand, only spare his life."
>
> So Satan departed from the presence of the LORD and struck Job with loathsome boils and agonizingly painful sores from the sole of his foot to the crown of his head. And Job took a piece of broken pottery with which to scrape himself, and he sat [down] among the ashes (rubbish heaps).
>
> —JOB 2:1–8

What amazes me is how God named Job and described him to Satan, saying, "Have you considered...*My servant* Job?" God keeps your name not only in the palm of His hand but also in His mouth. (See Isaiah 49:16; 43:1.) The devil and his demons are copycats, so they do something similar. They keep your name on their satanic lips, especially when you're trying to walk uprightly and reverently fear the Lord. You need to destroy every mention of your name by the devil and his demons. He doesn't name you to bless you. He puts sickness and premature death in the same sentence to steal your purpose and destiny. He releases a spirit of destruction and poverty over your name and unleashes his arsenals against you. It's time to take your name off the lips of Satan and every demon. It's time to baptize your name in the blood of Jesus.

HE WASHED MY NAME AND MADE ALL THINGS NEW

What I am about to say is only to give God glory. I am beyond grateful for what He has done in my life. My last name, Ramirez, was saturated with witchcraft and a demonic alcohol addiction that killed my father's father, who died as a drunk on the streets of Puerto Rico. That same devil trampled over my dad, who died from a gunshot wound to the head. That happened during a three-day alcohol spree that ended in a South Bronx social club. That is how it was with our bloodline.

I remember the night we received the news of my father's death. I was thirteen when my mother and I walked in the cold night rain and stood by the front door of the social club. My father lay dead on the other side of the door. The spirit of alcohol and premature death came for him that night.

The last name my father and I shared was caught up in the world of witchcraft. When I got saved, I didn't realize that the Lord redeemed my last name and washed it in Jesus' blood. Today, my name is known all over the world because Jesus Christ dismantled the hosts of hell and ripped my name out of their mouths. Then He brought my name into His kingdom.

In 2021, after I regained most of the eyesight I'd lost in a demonic attack, a Christian woman from China reached out on Facebook to ask how my eyes were doing.

I asked her, "Who are you?"

She said, "I live in Shanghai."

I answered, "I've never been there or preached there."

She said, "You don't have to. Your testimony has touched the underground church of Jesus Christ. Your last name is known all over China. There are 1.4 billion believers praying for you."

I was blown away by the goodness of Jesus Christ and all He has done for me. I'm praying today He does the same for you, scattering the satanic councils of the demonic world by the fire of the Holy Spirit. They will have to release your name from the kingdom of darkness, the incarceration of curses, and all witchcraft. Any works involving your name in satanic meetings and councils will be destroyed by the anointing and the fire of the Holy Spirit. In the mighty name of Jesus Christ, that includes every evil plan, plot, scheme, and wile that is set against you.

As you pray the following fire prayers, I believe complete destruction will come on every demonic and satanic element that is set against you and your family. Their last chance to accomplish anything against you has expired, in the mighty name of Jesus. You can tell the devil, "Stay where you are. We're coming for you."

Now let's pray.

FIRE PRAYERS

Father, I dip myself in the blood of Jesus, and I release a wall of fire on my name (Zech. 2:5). In Jesus' name, amen.

Let the angel of the Lord encamp around my name, my family's name, and my family's bloodline today. I break the forces of darkness, and I curse their schemes to the root. Let their plans shrivel up and die whenever my name is found in their camp. In the name of Jesus, amen.

Holy Spirit, recover my last name, my family's name, and my ministry's name. Remove them from the devil's hands, lips, and mouth. Wash these names in the blood of Jesus Christ, and make all things new. In Jesus' name, amen.

In the name of Jesus, I grab the sword of the Spirit, and I chop to pieces every stronghold, bondage, and entrapment of the devil that has wrapped itself around my name. My name is my inheritance. My name has purpose. My name has destiny. My name will fulfill everything God has called it to be. In Jesus' name, amen.

In Jesus' name, I break off my name from all demonic or satanic DNA that the devil has planted on it.

By the fire of God, I destroy any place in the demonic world where my name has been mentioned or incarcerated to remove my purpose and destiny. Let the Holy Spirit's fire burn down those places and release my name now, in the name of Jesus.

Let the lightning of the Holy Spirit smash every kind of satanic council and meeting. Let every demon that mentions my name go mute, in the name of Jesus.

In the name of Jesus, I destroy every demonic or satanic court that has mentioned my name.

I destroy every satanic jury that tries my name. Let them all be destroyed today, by the name of Jesus Christ.

In Jesus' name, I chop off the heads of every satanic judge that is trying to preside over my name.

In Jesus' name, let the Holy Spirit bring confusion on every demon that is trying to kidnap my name.

I break all curses, vexes, and voodoo over my name in the satanic realm of the spirit and the world of Satan. I dip arrows in the blood of Jesus to completely and fully destroy every altar that has my name assigned to it. In Jesus' name, I pray.

I dip myself and my last name, which represents my family's bloodline, in the blood of Jesus. I do the same for both sides of my family.

I release Zechariah 2:5, which says, "'For I,' declares the Lord, 'will be a wall of fire around {Jerusalem} [protecting her from enemies], and I will be the glory in her midst.'" I declare a wall of fire on my last name and my family's bloodline, with warring angels to protect our family's name, heritage, and inheritance, in Jesus' name.

I release the thunder of God to confuse the devil's camp. Let those who try to hold hostage my last name and heritage attack one another instead. I break every demonic arsenal. Let them shrivel up, die, and release my name now. In Jesus' name, I pray.

In the name of Jesus, my natural DNA will not define who I am in Christ, because I have new DNA. Lord Jesus, as Your redeemed, my last name has been purified, sanctified, and touched by the Holy Spirit. Therefore, I will do great things for You until You return. In Your mighty name, amen.

I give God all the glory, praise, and worship that are due Him. Thank You, Lord, for renewing my name, family, and bloodline to Your kingdom.

PART III

COVERING YOUR HOME, FAMILY, WELL-BEING, DESTINY, AND CHURCH

Chapter 23

DECLARATIONS AND BLESSINGS
OVER YOUR HOME

MY DEAR BROTHER or sister in Christ, we have already chased some demons, destroyed demonic altars and alignments, and taken authority over astral-projecting, diabolical objects, curses, vexes, and voodoo. We have stopped certain satanic and demonic infiltrations, and we have confronted the devil. We have acted in the spiritual realm to arrest works of darkness.

Many times we just talk about spiritual matters. Many preachers talk about the devil but never confront him head-on. Soon we will release prayer arsenals to drive out the demonic forces that are trying to steal, kill, and destroy the blessings, peace, and rest that belong in our homes. But first, it's time to arise in the unmatchable name of Jesus Christ to establish the truth of God's blessings over our homes. It's time for our Lord to reign and rule over our homes, marriages, and identities so we can make Him proud.

Let's begin by confessing three scriptures over our houses. The Word of God should be first in our homes; everything else is secondary. Wherever the Word of God reigns and rules, there will always be light, peace, and rest.

> The curse of the LORD is on the house of the wicked, but He blesses the home of the just and righteous.
>
> —PROVERBS 3:33

> Then my people will live in a peaceful surrounding, and in secure dwellings and in undisturbed resting places.
>
> —ISAIAH 32:18

> If it is unacceptable in your sight to serve the LORD, choose for yourselves this day whom you will serve: whether the gods which your fathers served that were on the other side of the River, or

the gods of the Amorites in whose land you live; but as for me and my house, we will serve the LORD.

—JOSHUA 24:15

As you pray the following fire prayers, please know that the word *home* applies to your living space, whether it is a home, an apartment, or another type of living arrangement.

FIRE PRAYERS

Father, in the name of Jesus, I thank You for the home that You have given my family and me—not only as our dwelling but also as a place of rest and peace.

I declare that my house and my family members will serve Jesus Christ all the days of our lives. There will be nothing missing and nothing broken in our home.

I declare that the glory of the Lord will reign and rule over my family and our dwelling place, all day, every day, in Jesus' name.

Just as the ark of the covenant brought blessing to the house of Obed-edom (1 Chron. 13:14), let the presence of the Lord Jesus Christ bless my home and my family.

Father, in the name of Jesus Christ, I declare Psalm 23:5 over my home: "You prepare a table before me in the presence of my enemies. You have anointed and refreshed my head with oil; my cup overflows."

I cover my home, protecting it from any disaster, earthquake, tornado, or fire, or any type of demonic destruction. These will never seize my home, in Jesus' name.

Let all demonic or satanic residue be kicked out of my home now, in Jesus' name.

By the name of Jesus Christ, I call my home to be blessed, completely and fully.

I speak prosperity, health, joy, peace, unity, and laughter over my home and my family, in Jesus' name.

I declare my home to be a pavilion of the Lord. I declare that the blessings of heaven will reign and rule over my home, in Jesus' name.

I speak by the power of the Holy Spirit to declare and decree that no evil report will come out of my dwelling, in the mighty name of Jesus.

I speak to the atmosphere of my home: be holy and filled with peace and joy in Jesus Christ.

I declare that embarrassments should not be known in my home, in Jesus' name.

I decree that poverty should not know my address, in Jesus' name.

No sickness of any kind will reign or rule over my home ever again, in Jesus' name.

Let the foundation of this dwelling be established in blessing, in the almighty name of Jesus Christ.

I bless my home completely and fully, inside and out, in the name that is above every name, King Jesus.

I speak blessings, health, prosperity, increase, abundance of rain, life, and no death over my home, my family, my friends, and anyone who visits my home. This place will be a reservoir of God's abundance, in Jesus' name.

Lord Jesus, You are welcome in my home always and forever. Hallelujah! Let Your presence fill my home, completely and fully, all day, every day. In Your mighty name, I pray.

Chapter 24

PRAYER ARSENALS TO DRIVE DEMONS OUT OF YOUR HOME

NOW WE WILL cover your home from every satanic or demonic entity, including devils, spirits, and ghosts. I don't care what you call them; they are not welcome and will not be made comfortable where you are. Someone may have lived in your home before you. Every satanic visitation of witchcraft and any practices of the kingdom of darkness that occurred before you moved in will be destroyed and unable to bring darkness, discord, division, sickness, poverty, entrapment, delays, premature death, divorce devils, confusion, or chaos. Today you will serve an eviction notice like none they have ever seen.

Our homes always need to welcome Jesus Christ. Let them be houses of prayer, not dwellings that darkness and demons would enjoy. Let's remove any physical and spiritual clutter. The devil loves clutter and disorganization. When I was doing witchcraft to families, some of my prime targets were homes that were cluttered, dirty, or even filthy. I preferred homes that had boxes and clothes everywhere. Believe it or not, demons hide in those places.

Another type of house I favored was a divided house, where winning an argument and having the last word were important. By the words of the residents' own mouths, I gained the legal right to send demons to torment their marriage or children. The same was true of homes where profanity and ungodly television shows or movies were front and center. I sent lust and perversion spirits to destroy those homes.

TIME TO CLEAN HOUSE IN JESUS' NAME

I remember when I was young in my Christian faith and was invited to share my testimony at a Christian elementary/junior high school—not a worldly school but a Christian school. Many parents panicked because an ex-satanist was going to speak to their children. For the day of the event, parents took off from work and signed permission slips to allow their kids to hear my testimony. As the event played out, I realized a sad truth: many of those believers had no idea what their everyday choices were accomplishing in the spirit realm.

The auditorium was filled that day, with standing room only. The Holy Spirit told me to share my testimony on a level the children could receive, and He moved on those young people and their parents in amazing ways, maybe like never before. They are still thanking the Lord Jesus Christ for bringing Evangelist John Ramirez to their school. Why? Because the devil had been made comfortable in their homes. The parents had allowed their children to be indoctrinated by Harry Potter books and movies and the demonic Twilight series, which involves werewolves. My visit was their wake-up call.

After I spoke, those families could not believe the filth they had allowed in their homes or the legal rights they had given the devil. About a week later I started receiving letters from young people who thanked me for exposing the devil. Their parents filled up garbage bags with Harry Potter paraphernalia, including the posters they stripped from the walls of their children's rooms. Then they rededicated those rooms to Jesus Christ. Those kids were set free. They were on fire for the Lord Jesus Christ because God loves the children.

What is in your home today? If Jesus Christ dropped in, would He be comfortable there? Would He be pleased with your home's appearance and with your stuff? Would the wall hangings and other items please Him? Would He approve of whatever is in your closets? Or do certain items attract demonic forces to your home and give them permission to destroy what God is trying to build?

I always say, "Church starts at home, not in the building you visit on Sundays." The devil doesn't like that idea. He gets upset about what you are about to do—you are going to purify and sanctify your home, children, relationships, and marriage. You are going to rededicate them to the Lord Jesus Christ.

I rejoice with you because you're about to tell the devil, "You don't live here anymore. It's time for you to leave my house." Go ahead and send him packing with the powerful fire prayers I have provided for you. Put him on the run, and slam the door shut behind him. Tell him, "Not my house. Not my children. Not my marriage. I dedicate everything back to the Lord Jesus Christ *today.*"

When you have completed the fire prayers, take a few minutes to anoint the doors, windows, and walls of your home. Anoint the furniture and all your family members, in the mighty name of Jesus Christ. Let your home be a house of prayer and let David's words encourage you: "I have been young and now I am old, yet I have not seen the righteous (those in right standing with God) abandoned or his descendants pleading for bread" (Ps. 37:25).

FIRE PRAYERS

I wash my home with the blood of Jesus Christ, from top to bottom and from side to side.

With the blood of Jesus Christ, I paint my house red in the Spirit.

Let the foundations of my home now be dedicated to the Lord Jesus Christ.

If any demons, warlocks, or witches lived in this home before I did, I serve them an eviction notice right now, in the name of Jesus Christ.

If my home contains any type of witchcraft altar, candle lighting, or incense burning, let it be destroyed by the blood of Jesus today.

If any kind of demonic forces contaminated my home, I serve them an eviction notice today, in Jesus' precious name.

If anyone committed murder, rape, incest, or bestiality in this home before I moved in, let it be destroyed by the blood of Jesus.

If anyone conducted séances, witchcraft practices, or occult practices in my home at any time, let them be destroyed, completely and fully, in Jesus' name.

If anyone known or unknown is sending witchcraft to my home, or if there is any demon visitation, let them drown in the blood of Jesus now, in Jesus' name.

I destroy every astral-projecting devil who has come into my home or is trying to come into my home. I cut the silver cord (the contract between an astral-projecting person and the demon). Let it be destroyed, in Jesus' name.

If any human sacrifices of any kind have been offered in this home, let that innocent blood be washed away, in Jesus' name.

If any diabolical dedications or celebrations have occurred in my home, let them be destroyed, in Jesus' name.

If any cursed object has occupied or been displayed in this home, I bring it down, in the name of Jesus.

I bind every evil spirit in this room, and I command them to leave now, in Jesus' name.

Today, I cover the rooms of my home and everything they contain in the blood of Jesus.

Let every demon that has invaded any room of my home catch fire in the spirit realm. Let these demons burn to ashes, never to return, in the name of Jesus Christ.

I rededicate my home to Father God, King Jesus, and the Holy Spirit, in Jesus' name.

I put the blood of the Lamb on every wall, window, and door in every room of this place. I put warring angels in my dwelling to guard the north, south, east, and west of my home, in Jesus' name.

I declare and decree that my home should be a house of prayer, in Jesus' name.

I remove from my home every foul and wicked spirit that has made itself comfortable because of my words or has entered my home through any open door or gateway. By the fire of the Holy Spirit, I burn them out.

Let every shadow and power of the dark side in my home be destroyed, dismantled, and uprooted now, in Jesus' name.

I break and destroy every bit of legal ground I have granted to any demons through my dreams or through any demonic practices in my home. Let them be destroyed now, in Jesus' mighty name.

I break every cursed object that was buried in my home, either before or after I moved here. If anyone has placed such an object here, let the fire of God burn it out now. In Jesus' name, amen.

In Jesus' name, I dismantle every altar in the spirit realm that has my home address on it.

By the fire of the Holy Spirit, I purify my home, fully and completely, in Jesus' name. I take back my home from the forces of darkness and the devil himself, and I dedicate it back to Jesus Christ. Amen.

I bind the strongman that is over my family, my home, and these rooms. I command the strongman to leave, in the name of Jesus.

Let every evil doorkeeper that is trying to control or manipulate in my home be destroyed today by the blood of Jesus Christ.

I dedicate my family back to Jesus Christ. I dedicate the foundations of this home to Jesus Christ. I dedicate all the rooms in my home to Jesus Christ. Holy Spirit, You are welcome in this place. Holy Spirit, purify and sanctify my home and marriage, my children and their rooms and clothing, every closet, and the attic. In the name of Jesus, amen.

I break all curses that have been working against my property and against what I own, including my car. In Jesus' name, amen.

I pray out of my home and my vehicles all premature deaths and accidents of all kinds. I pray this in the mighty name of Jesus Christ. Amen.

Let every satanic spirit that is attached to those who visit my home be destroyed and removed from my house, in Jesus' name.

Thank You, Lord, for keeping this home and keeping all who live here, in Jesus' name.

Chapter 25

ARSENAL PRAYERS WHEN MOVING INTO A HOME OR APARTMENT

I LEARNED SOMETHING THROUGH my travels: *always* pray for your hotel room. You don't know what kind of spirits are there. Fornication and other ungodly things happen in hotels. Adulterous and other perverse spirits hang around, waiting to seize an opportunity to triumph over the next person who stays in the room.

The same is true for apartments and pre-owned homes. Before you move in, it is important to take authority over any demonic issues and evict any spirits that were allowed to take residence under a previous renter or owner. We always need to be armed and dangerous, spiritually alert, and sober minded (1 Pet. 5:8). The devil has many ways to steal, kill, and destroy. God warned us to be wise, saying, "My people are destroyed for lack of knowledge" (Hos. 4:6). It's time to use wisdom and be spiritually smart against the enemy of our souls.

Before you move into your new place, make a spiritual assessment. Then use the fire prayers in this chapter as heaven's arsenal to destroy every despicable demon, any form of witchcraft, or any other foul thing that entered that home before it was yours. Every place has a history, and the history of your new home or apartment might need to be turned around.

As the Holy Spirit leads, continue to dedicate and assess your home. Take spiritual inventory of everything and everyone involved. This establishes and keeps the foundations of your dwelling place, along with your marriage, children, and loved ones. Remain mindful that the Lord Jesus Christ gave you the place. Continue to be sober minded about that. Ask Him to give you the revelation and clarity you need to maintain and cultivate His blessings. Let no devil, portal, or gateway contaminate the place ever again, in Jesus' name.

Now go ahead and shake the foundations of your living space or hotel room with these fire prayers. Let the devil know he's no longer welcome there.

FIRE PRAYERS

Today, I stand in my home with the authority that Jesus Christ has given me over every lingering demon and devil that was invited into this place, whether consciously or unconsciously. It's time for you to go where the Lord sends you. In Jesus' name, amen.

Today I serve an eviction notice on every black shadow or spirit that is trying to bring fear and torment into this place. I command it to leave now, never to return. In the mighty name of Jesus Christ, amen.

Today I command every evil night-stalking devil that has visited this home to leave. By the blood of Jesus, I serve you with an eviction notice. I command every familial spirit that is here now or has been here at any time in the past to go, in the name of Jesus.

I destroy completely every poltergeist devil that has come in through the one-eyed monster called television. In the name of Jesus, I destroy any filth that was entertained here, including sexual content, profanity, and blasphemy. I command all of it to leave now, in Jesus' name.

By the blood of Jesus, I serve an eviction notice to every demonic influence and wicked spirit that made their home in this place. In Jesus' name, amen.

I break, destroy, dismantle, and uproot every curse, vex, voodoo, and occult practice that was performed in this place through any persons or families. I command their works and any residue to leave now, in the mighty name of Jesus Christ.

I curse to the root every demonic night-stalking devil spirit that visits my dreams, walks around this home, stalks my family, or stands by my bedside at night. I command it to leave now, in Jesus' name.

I call on the Holy Spirit to release the fire of heaven on every devil that has made its home in this place. Let Your fire burn all of them to ashes, in Jesus' name.

In the mighty name of Jesus Christ, I shut up, shut down, and kick out every evil spirit that has contaminated this place and seeks to destroy my marriage, child(ren), family, or loved ones by bringing discord, division, or arguments out of nowhere.

I release the fire of heaven on every demon that was sent here through witchcraft, spoken words, ungodly acts, and any doors and portals that were opened by any previous occupants of this place. I smite them with the blood of Jesus on their heads and command them to leave now, in Jesus' name.

In Jesus' name, I command every sexual spirit and adulterous fornication spirit lingering in my hotel room to leave now.

Every spirit of suicide or fear that has made itself comfortable in this place, I command you to leave now, in the name of Jesus Christ.

I cover every door, window, wall, and floor and all furniture in this place with the blood of Jesus Christ.

In Jesus' name, I ask the Holy Spirit to release the anointing and fire of God in this place today.

I declare and decree that as they enter, I anoint in the Spirit every person who walks into my home, in the unmatchable name of Jesus Christ.

I release warring angels into this place, to protect everyone and everything in it, in Jesus' name.

I release the fire of the Holy Spirit from the north, south, east, and west to vacate and evict every kind of demon from this place, in Jesus' name.

Today and forevermore, I dedicate this place to Jehovah, the Most High God. Let His presence dwell and rule here. In the mighty name of Jesus Christ, amen.

Chapter 26

PRAYERS AGAINST DEMONS THAT DESTROY MARRIAGES

NEXT, WE ARE going to take authority over every satanic divorce devil, all spiritual divorce papers, and every plot of the devil to steal our marriages. We are going to destroy every altar of the satanic kingdom that has our names on it. We will also annihilate all kinds of spirit husbands, spirit wives, and spirits of manipulation, adultery, lust, infidelity, and perversion that the devil wants to release on our marriages. The devil is going to back off because we're coming for him.

The devil despises the godly union of marriage that symbolizes the relationship between Jesus Christ and His bride, the church. But we are about to take authority over anything Satan might use to pollute and fracture our families and inheritance. That includes drugs, alcohol, poverty, and any other struggles he uses to dismantle marriages.

Recent studies have shown that divorce rates among couples who are committed Christians are lower than the rates among nominal Christians or unbelievers.[1] Still, divorce wreaks havoc on Christian marriages. Hindrances, delays, blockages, and distractions happen in married life. Married believers need to fight the good fight *together* and remain in agreement with each other. There is power in agreement, and unity keeps a marriage strong.

Trust me on this: the grass is not greener on the other side. Any person you think should replace your spouse could have more demonic issues than the person you leave behind. When I was a warlock for hire, I would hit marriages with something we called the 80/20. The 80 represents a person's current spouse, who was "only" 80 percent. What our target wanted was a 100 percent husband or wife. But nobody is 100 percent, except God.

Once the target started shopping around, my goal was to make a 20 percent option look good. When someone is traveling on demonic highways to search for "something better," it's easy to dupe them. It's like the story of the dog at the edge of the lake with a bone in his mouth. He sees the bone reflected in the water and thinks it looks better than the one he's got. So he releases the real bone and tries to grab the one that caught his eye. But there is no bone. It's all smoke and mirrors.

When people become dissatisfied with their spouses and lust for "something better," the devil tries to oblige by giving them delusional spirits about individuals who look like better mates. The devil starts the ball rolling with discouragement, doubt, division, and discord in a marriage. The strategy preys on whatever weaknesses a discontented spouse already has, such as pornography, lust, perversion, alcohol, drugs, or even financial lack. The devil exploits those gateways and destroys the marriage.

The devil pulls this bait and switch countless times every day. Unsuspecting people drop the 80 percent God gave them for the 20 percent the devil dishes up on the street. That's how the devil destroys homes and people's unity with Christ. He destroys marriage covenants that were made in the eyes of God. And in exchange he offers discontented people something less than what they had.

It's time to fight and take back your home. It's time to entrust your marriage to God's perfect will. When He puts two people together, He knows what's best. Remember that the stormy seasons in marriage don't last forever. Don't make permanent decisions based on temporary situations. I thank God I have learned not to do that. I realize that the devil's strategy is to make spouses feel that they need to have the last word or make the last argument to prove a point. But why win the argument or prove your point only to lose your marriage?

Marriage is not about who is right or wrong, who wins the argument, or who has the last word. The Bible says, "Therefore humble yourselves [demote, lower yourselves in your own estimation] under the mighty hand of God, that in due time He may exalt you" (1 Pet. 5:6, AMPC). Second Corinthians 10:5 says to "refute arguments and theories and reasonings and every proud and lofty thing that sets itself up against the [true] knowledge of God; and...lead every thought and purpose away captive into the obedience of Christ (the Messiah, the Anointed One)" (AMPC). And Ephesians 6:12 warns that "we are not wrestling with flesh and blood [contending only with physical opponents], but against the despotisms, against the powers, against [the master spirits who are] the world rulers of this present darkness, against the spirit forces of wickedness in the heavenly (supernatural) sphere" (AMPC).

Now let's refute the devil's delusions and pray. Confess anything that is hindering your marriage. Release and destroy it, knowing that every demon, principality, stronghold, and strongman that is trying to destroy your marriage must bow to the name of Jesus (Phil. 2:10–11). When you release Jesus' name and disown all hindrances, curse them to the root and let them shrivel up and die. They will have no more dominion over your marriage, your family, or anything the devil is trying to use against you. Once and for all, issue the eviction notice by the blood of Jesus Christ, the finished work of the cross, God's promises, and His Word.

Fire Prayers

Father, I destroy the cankerworm and the locust that are trying to eat away at my marriage (Joel 2:25, KJV). In the name of Jesus, amen.

In the name of Jesus Christ, I destroy every plot, evil scheme, argument, and entrapment the devil is using to try and destroy my marriage.

In the name of Jesus, I destroy every demonic force and demon that is trying to frustrate my marriage.

In Jesus' name, I destroy all demonic discord and division that is attacking my marriage.

In the name of Jesus, let every known and unknown satanic power or activity that is working against my marriage die and shrivel up, completely and fully.

In the name of Jesus, I break every divorce paper in the spirit realm that has my name and my spouse's name on it.

In the name of Jesus Christ, I destroy every demonic dream that tries to take down our marriage. Let all of them drown in the blood of Jesus Christ.

Today, by the fire of God, I destroy every husband spirit and every wife spirit. In Jesus' name, amen.

In the name of Jesus, I destroy every pornography spirit, lust spirit, and perversion spirit that is trying to come against me and my marriage.

In Jesus' name, I break the spirits of poverty, perversion, and alcohol and every demonic weakness that is trying to incarcerate my marriage.

Right now, in the name of Jesus, I destroy the spirits of Jezebel and Delilah that are trying to come against my marriage.

In Jesus' name, I destroy the spirit of Ahab—that complacent devil that is trying to paralyze my marriage.

Let the judgment of God fall on every entrapment, open door, and open portal that the enemy has entered, including those involving legal rights that I or my spouse have given him. We destroy those things and return to God's perfect will for our marriage. In Jesus' name, amen.

Father, forgive us for any known and unknown sins we have committed against one another. Forgive any demonic and divorce words that we have spoken into the atmosphere. Let them all be destroyed. Father, purify us, our marriage, and our marriage papers, completely and fully. Let unity fill our home. Make it a place where two can put ten thousand to flight (Deut. 32:30). We are in agreement, as there is power in agreement. Let our marriage be sanctified and filled with the Holy Spirit, who is the center of our marriage, in Jesus' name. Give us wisdom, knowledge, revelation, and clarity in our spiritual walk together. Command a blessing over our home (Deut. 28:8), in the unmatchable name of Jesus Christ. Amen.

Lord, I give You praise and glory. I worship You and thank You, in Jesus' name. Amen.

Chapter 27

SPIRITUAL WARFARE DECLARATIONS OVER YOUR CHILDREN

As PARENTS WHO love our children, we need to remember that God is not done with them yet. If they are still on this earth, we are to stand with them, regardless of their ages. God forbid that we throw in the towel and give up on our kids. God never gave up on us. As I like to say, "Never give up on anybody. Miracles happen every day." Let's live expecting God to open the windows of heaven and pour out miracles over our families. I believe in my heart that He can do it in any given moment. I have seen miracles, signs, and wonders happen in my daughter's life, even when I couldn't see God's hand moving.

Before you hear the miracles, I need to explain how the testimony started. When my ex-wife and I divorced at a young age, my daughter was two years old. I loved her with all my heart and never stopped loving her. Many times I promised to come over the weekend and take her out for ice cream or a movie. Remember that I was a devil worshipper at the time, not a born-again believer. My little girl would wait by the window for hours, and her daddy never showed up. I am sorry to say that it happened often. I was more committed to the devil and his kingdom than to my own child. My actions brought trauma into her young life.

Fast-forward to years later, when Jesus Christ became my Lord and Savior. My daughter and I had remained in communication on and off. Once, she asked me if she could come live with me because she had a job opportunity in the city. I agreed, and she stayed with me for about eight months. It became the most diabolical time we ever shared.

I will not justify or excuse my behavior. I take full responsibility for my part in the pain she suffered as a child. The turmoil we faced during her eight months at my house was an attack from the pit of hell, and I knew it.

When she left my home to return to upstate New York, she was hurt and angry with me, and I was broken. I used to get up at three o'clock every morning and take an hour ride to watch her commute from upstate New York. Without her knowing it, I watched over her and tried to protect her. Then I would cry all the way back home.

Sometime later, God did a miracle. I prayed, fasted, and believed Him and His promise that I and my household would serve the Lord (Josh. 24:15). God completely restored my relationship with my daughter, and today it is supernaturally blessed. We pray together and talk about Jesus, and every time she needs me, I am there. I don't miss a beat. By the hand of Jesus Christ, I have become the daddy she always needed.

I pray that wherever you are today, you will believe God to keep writing your family's story. Don't lose hope. Don't lose faith. Now is the time to fight and show the devil that he tried messing with the wrong house.

Before you declare the fire prayers, confess these scriptures:

> Before I formed you in the womb I knew you [and approved of you as My chosen instrument], and before you were born I consecrated you [to Myself as My own]; I have appointed you as a prophet to the nations.
>
> —JEREMIAH 1:5

> All your [spiritual] sons will be disciples [of the LORD], and great will be the well-being of your sons.
>
> —ISAIAH 54:13

> Train up a child in the way he should go [teaching him to seek God's wisdom and will for his abilities and talents], even when he is old he will not depart from it.
>
> —PROVERBS 22:6

FIRE PRAYERS

In the name of Jesus, heavens be opened over my child(ren) and their child(ren), today and forevermore. Favor of God, please be their portion all the rest of their lives. In Jesus' name, amen.

My child(ren) will be the head and not the tail (Deut. 28:13).

My child(ren) will run and not be weary; they will walk and not faint (Isa. 40:31, NKJV). *Their portion will always be blessed and in the hands of our Lord Jesus Christ.*

I declare over my child(ren) that they will always be blessed financially so they can further the kingdom of Jesus Christ, provide for their families, and protect them, in Jesus' name.

In Jesus' name, I destroy, completely and fully, every demonic door of hindrance, delay, blockage, and distraction that is trying to come on my kid(s). They will live under heaven's open door all the days of their lives, in Jesus' name.

In Jesus' name, my child(ren) will enter 100 percent God-fearing marriages.

My child(ren) will not pursue any of the enemy's plots, schemes, or wiles. They will live out their purpose and destinies, in Jesus' name.

My child(ren)'s names will be great on the earth, in Jesus' name.

I prophesy over my child(ren) that they will never see a day of sickness or backsliding, in Jesus' name.

Let every demonic plot or entrapment of the enemy that would try to incarcerate my child(ren) be destroyed completely and fully so they are free, from the tops of their heads to the soles of their feet. Let no bloodline or generational curse hinder my child(ren) from being raised up in the Lord and finishing their course. In Jesus' name, amen.

My child(ren) will not inherit poverty but will be mighty men and women of God, in Jesus' name.

In Jesus' name, I curse to the root every premature death, sickness, bondage, and fornication devil that is trying to take my child(ren) down.

Father, in the name of Jesus, let my child(ren) find Your favor in every season of their lives.

Let my child(ren) be filled with the Holy Spirit, completely and fully, all the days of their lives, in Jesus' name.

Let every evil eye and all jealousy, envy, and hatred from the north, south, east, and west be destroyed from my child(ren)'s friendships, peers, families, or any person who tries to come against them, in Jesus' name.

In Jesus' name, I break every satanic friendship from the streets and schools that is trying to manipulate and control my child(ren).

I destroy every kind of demonic influence or deception that is trying to incarcerate my child(ren). I destroy these evils, completely and fully, in Jesus' name.

In Jesus' name, I destroy any kind of satanic or demonic friendship that is trying to sidetrack my child(ren).

In Jesus' name, let every vagabond devil that is trying to pursue and control my child(ren) be destroyed.

I release my child(ren), nephews, and nieces from any demonic or satanic arrest, in Jesus' name.

I speak revelation and clarity over my child(ren), in the name of Jesus.

I release the Spirit of God on my child(ren) who are lost and in the world. Lord, bring them back to the cross of Jesus Christ.

In Jesus' name, I destroy and break off my child(ren) every backsliding spirit that would try to rob their purpose, destiny, and relationship with almighty God.

I curse to the root every hindrance, delay, blockage, and distraction that is trying to come on my child(ren), nephews, and nieces. They will inherit the blessings of the kingdom, in Jesus' name.

I curse to the root every sickness, bloodline curse, and demonic family curse that is trying to destroy my child(ren). Let it shrivel up and die. Let the blessings of the Lord be on, in, and through my child(ren), in Jesus' name.

Thank You, Lord, for my child(ren). Thank You for sealing their futures, purposes, and destinies in the hands of almighty God. In Jesus' name, I pray. Amen.

Chapter 28

POWERFUL PRAYERS TO PROTECT YOUR CHILDREN FROM DEMONIC ATTACKS

COVERING OUR CHILDREN in prayer means covering not only their well-being but also the fulfillment of their purposes and destinies in God. Matthew 18:6 says that "whoever causes one of these little ones who believe in Me to stumble and sin [by leading him away from My teaching], it would be better for him to have a heavy millstone [as large as one turned by a donkey] hung around his neck and to be drowned in the depth of the sea." When we pray, we take this warning to heart.

Abraham was an amazing man of God. In his lifetime he was very rich. Yet he was sad because he was childless. Abraham thought generationally. He wanted to pass his legacy to his children and his children's children. It hurt him to think the good things God gave him would not extend to his own bloodline. So Abraham (then called Abram) cried out to God for a son.

> Abram said, "Lord GOD, what reward will You give me, since I am [leaving this world] childless, and he who will be the owner and heir of my house is this [servant] Eliezer from Damascus?" And Abram continued, "Since You have given no child to me, one (a servant) born in my house is my heir." Then behold, the word of the LORD came to him, saying, "This man [Eliezer] will not be your heir but he who shall come from your own body shall be your heir." And the LORD brought Abram outside [his tent into the night] and said, "Look now toward the heavens and count the stars—if you are able to count them." Then He said to him, "So [numerous] shall your descendants be." Then Abram believed in (affirmed, trusted in, relied on, remained steadfast to) the LORD; and He counted (credited) it to him as righteousness (doing right in regard to God and man).
>
> —GENESIS 15:2–6

Even with his polluted, toxic mind, the devil also thinks generationally. Through Christ Jesus our families receive generational blessings. Through Satan they receive generational curses. He hungers to get his filthy hands on our children. He wants to steal their inheritances and destroy their futures.

It's time to fight back. Our children are under the most diabolical attack ever in their lives. Authority figures in the schools seem to want to brainwash them, from elementary school all the way through college. Atheist professors work to break our children's wills and reshape their characters and identities in ways that please hell. They are trying to hijack our children's innocence and confuse them with suggestions of homosexuality, lesbianism, and bisexuality. "You can choose any gender you want," they say. It is a despicable attack from the pit of hell. It is up to us to expose it, guard our children, and strip away the false labels the enemy wants them to accept. But sadly, much of the church is allowing the devil to censor and silence its voice.

THE DEVIL WORKS OVERTIME

The devil is operating in every way and on every level against our children. It doesn't matter whether they are being raised in good homes. The devil is working to infiltrate all our homes, schools, colleges, and the rest of society. He uses television and other media to hijack young minds. He even uses "family-friendly" channels to do his work. Filth is everywhere. Movies such as the Harry Potter franchise seduce our kids with magic and sexual content. Our kids are being taught that sex outside marriage is normal and that they can sleep around with as many people as they desire. News outlets celebrate abortion rights and tell our children they don't need their parents' consent, permission, or blessing to arrange for abortions and gender transitions. They are urged to do whatever seems right in their own eyes (Judg. 21:25).

Many children are going through what I experienced growing up. Those who should be protecting them are sacrificing them to the satanic world. Satan also uses social media, music, and different demonic and occult practices to incarcerate them in one way or another. It is diabolical, and it is happening, whether we know it or not.

Yet I have more bad news for the devil: we will fight the good fight and reclaim our children for the Lord Jesus Christ—not only their identities and purposes but also their relationships with almighty God. We will do this keeping the following scriptures in mind:

> Behold, children are a heritage and gift from the LORD, the fruit of the womb a reward. Like arrows in the hand of a warrior, so are the children of one's youth. How blessed [happy and fortunate] is the man whose quiver is filled with them; they will not be ashamed when they speak with their enemies [in gatherings] at the [city] gate.
>
> —Psalm 127:3–5

> May he bring justice to the poor among the people, save the children of the needy and crush the oppressor.
>
> —Psalm 72:4

Now pray for your children the way Hannah prayed for Samuel. (See 1 Samuel 1:10–15.). Whatever their ages, whether they are male or female, surrender them to the Lord. Rededicate them to Him, and they will become great ministers, prophets, teachers, evangelists, pastors, entrepreneurs, doctors, lawyers, teachers, firefighters, police officers—whatever the Lord ordains them to be. They will stand on the platforms God has created for them, and they will represent Jesus Christ. They will live and not die. Their days will not be cut short. They will declare the works of the Lord. (See Psalm 118:17; 91:16.) They will not be sick or backslide. They will hold on to their innocence until God brings the Boaz or Esther that He has chosen for them, in Jesus' name.

As you pray the fire prayers, expect every despicable demonic or satanic door that has tempted your children to be closed completely and fully, regardless of the demonic weapons the enemy has used against them. You are serving an eviction notice to the devil and his demons, and it will uproot and permanently destroy every attack that is underway.

Fire Prayers

In the name of Jesus, I baptize all my child(ren) in His precious blood.

In Jesus' name, I baptize all my child(ren) in the fire of the Holy Spirit.

Let all known and unknown satanic manipulation of my child(ren) be completely and fully destroyed, in Jesus' name.

In the mighty name of Jesus, I destroy every demonic plot, scheme, and wile that the devil has put on my child(ren).

I hide my child(ren) in the cleft of the rock (Exod. 33:22; Ps. 27:5), far from every scheme, wile, and plot of the devil.

I break off from my child(ren) all brainwashing, all satanic entrapment, and every false identity of homosexuality, perversion, or pornography, in Jesus' name.

I destroy my child(ren)'s addiction to satanic content on television, in books, and on social media. Let all of it be destroyed, once and for all, in Jesus' name.

Let every devil operating via social media (be specific) shrivel up and die today, in Jesus' name.

I destroy every satanic sickness that has come on my child(ren), whether it is cancer, diabetes, high blood pressure, or any other demonic infirmity. Let it be annihilated, in Jesus' name.

I destroy every satanic program, movie, sitcom, or television show involving magic, false identities, cursing, and blasphemy that has entertained my child(ren) through the eye gates or ear gates. Let any diabolical lines they have repeated from any movie or TV program be destroyed by the blood of Jesus.

I break every satanic scheme that keeps my child(ren) addicted to electronic devices, including tablets and cell phones. I destroy all mechanisms that have manipulated or brainwashed them by infiltrating their minds, souls, and thinking. Let it all drown in the blood of Jesus. Amen.

By the fire of the Holy Spirit, I destroy and cancel all programming, satanic alignment, and infiltrations that have fed my child(ren). Today I break, destroy, and uproot them all, in Jesus' name.

By the fire of the Holy Spirit, I burn every satanic birth certificate, spiritual adoption, and false identity that adopts my child(ren) into the kingdom of darkness. Let these devices be burned and destroyed, in Jesus' name.

Let every personal item that belongs to my home or my child(ren) (including young children, teenagers, and adults of all ages) *and is found on any satanic altar in the spirit realm be abolished and destroyed. In the name of Jesus, amen.*

I put on notice every demonic power, and I cut the ropes of those who are acting as my child(ren)'s puppeteers on behalf of the enemy's agenda. I do this in the mighty, untouchable name of Jesus Christ.

I break and destroy every evil related to oppression, depression, suicide, or demonic addiction that has come on my child(ren). Let it be broken off them completely, in Jesus' mighty name.

I break off my child(ren) every false identity spoken over their lives through my mouth or any other mouth. Let those words drown in the blood of Jesus today.

I destroy repeating patterns and cycles by which my child(ren) is(are) freed in one season only to be bound in the next. In Jesus' name, I destroy these schemes. They are never to return or threaten my child(ren)'s inheritance again.

Father, I put my child(ren) in Your mighty right hand. No devil, hell, witch, vex, social media, television program, or movie will be able to recruit them. In Jesus' mighty name, I pray.

In Jesus' name, my child(ren) will not be married to any entrapments of the devil, including any commitments or agreements made with the enemy of their soul(s) or with his kingdom, now or in the future.

Holy Spirit, please hold my child(ren), from the crowns of their heads to the soles of their feet. Cover them and keep them from turning in any direction that does not serve their purposes and destinies, in Jesus' name.

I declare and decree over my child(ren) a wall of fire on their minds, hearts, spirits, and souls (Zech. 2:5), in the mighty name of Jesus Christ.

I destroy every generational curse in every branch of my bloodline that will hinder my child(ren)'s walk with the Lord Jesus Christ in any way. Let all generational curses be uprooted all the way back to Adam and Eve, in Jesus' name.

Father, in Jesus' precious name, I give you back the pen with which to write the rest of my child(ren)'s stories. Let their destinies and purposes be written as masterpieces and best sellers that bring glory and honor to Your name.

Chapter 29

PRAYERS FOR STUDENTS TO BE SUCCESSFUL

I N THE PREVIOUS chapter we talked about the enemy's attacks on our children through the educational system. We have seen that students who stand for righteousness and resist or oppose these satanic strategies are persecuted. Their grades can be negatively affected, and some are made unwelcome. Some are even asked to leave their schools and colleges.

We cannot sugarcoat this issue. People are being persecuted because they believe and put their trust in King Jesus. The fire prayers in this chapter are for students—not only college or trade school students but also elementary, junior high/middle school, and high school students who don't want to shrink back from the Lord when they enter the devil's territory.

Encourage your children to pray these prayers. (You can adjust the wording where needed for younger children.) But first, help them meditate on these scriptures:

> He who has begun a good work in you will complete it until the day of Jesus Christ.
>
> —PHILIPPIANS 1:6, NKJV

> In all these things we are more than conquerors through Him who loved us.
>
> —ROMANS 8:37, NKJV

> I can do all things through Christ who strengthens me.
>
> —PHILIPPIANS 4:13, NKJV

Now let's dress for battle and pray.

FIRE PRAYERS

May the peace of God that surpasses all understanding rest on me at school today (Phil. 4:7). Let the peace of the Holy Spirit rest on my mind during every examination for my diploma, certificate, or degree, in Jesus' name.

I declare that I have a sound mind in Christ Jesus, today and forevermore (2 Tim. 1:7).

Father, as I stand in this educational institution, I trust You to be with me. No weapon that is formed against me through my teachers or professors will prosper (Isa. 54:17). In the name of Jesus, I declare and decree that I will complete my course and make Jesus Christ proud.

In the name of Jesus, I break off and destroy every spirit of fear and anxiety that any professor or teacher is trying to put on me through any form of intimidation.

I break off and destroy every demonic, unrighteous word that is spoken in my classroom to pierce my ears and spirit and contaminate or brainwash me in any way. Let those words be destroyed, in the name of Jesus Christ.

I rebuke every satanic or demonic plot, scheme, or wile from any teacher or professor who tries to indoctrinate me in the devil's demonic theology. Let it be destroyed, in Jesus' name.

In the name of Jesus and by His blood, I destroy every wicked spirit that is trying to distract me from my exams, studies, or classroom activities.

In Jesus' name, I destroy every devil and demon that is trying to steal the wisdom and knowledge that I will use to pass any exams or tests that I need to complete my diploma or degree.

Lord, I thank You for bringing to my remembrance the information I need for every examination, throughout my education, in the name of Jesus. Holy Spirit, please help me to pass my tests, graduate, and make Jesus Christ proud.

I plead the blood of Jesus over every exam, paper, term paper, quiz, and other course requirement. Help me to achieve the grade that God intends. It will not be altered or edited by any professor or teacher in any way, shape, or form. In Jesus' name, amen.

In Jesus' name, I destroy every entrapment of the devil in any classroom setting that would target me or endanger my diploma or degree.

Lord, I thank You for making me the head and not the tail (Deut. 28:13). In the name of Jesus, amen.

In Christ Jesus alone, I will succeed in everything I do. I will not fail but will complete the course that is part of my purpose and my destiny. In Jesus's name, I pray.

Lord, I give You praise and worship, knowing the good work I started back in elementary school continues now that I am in college (2 Tim. 3:14–17). You will bring it to completion and continue to lead me. No weapon, person, or devil will stop what you, the Almighty, have started. I will finish the course and make Jesus Christ proud that He picked me.

Chapter 30

PRAYERS TO DESTROY SATANIC SICKNESSES AND DECLARE HEALING IN JESUS' NAME

PEOPLE IN THE body of Christ are going through all kinds of demonic sicknesses. Some are generational, like the cancer devil that creeps into your family's bloodline. Some of us have seen cancer take out a grandmother, auntie, mother, and daughter all in the same family. Other families are dealing with diabetes, high blood pressure, or immune disorders. Even oppression and depression have plagued some families in the body of Christ. Too many of our precious brothers and sisters have suicidal thoughts. Members of their families have killed themselves, and now that demon has wrapped itself around them. It's time to cleanse any bloodlines that Satan has infected and purge these infirmities, once and for all.

I believe most sicknesses are satanic or demonic and are meant to compromise or destroy people's bodies. Because we carry the mind of Christ, our bodies (including our minds) are the temples of the Holy Spirit. God has blessed us with good doctors who are instrumental in our health at some level.

But there's something I don't understand about when doctors say, "This medication will make you better." If the medication is supposed to make you better or heal you, why do you need refills? There is nothing wrong with medication. Medications are made from ingredients God created. But we need to put our trust and our faith in the healing power of Jesus Christ that is on us, in us, and through us—even while we take medication for a season. I believe that infirmity spirits are demonic and that there is no reason to medicate them. It's time to cast them out.

We need to destroy this entrapment once and for all. It's time to live the lives God has called us to live as healthy people who are free and victorious, from the crowns of our heads to the soles of our feet. We need to declare healing over ourselves, our families, and our loved ones, in the mighty name of Jesus Christ.

Before you start attacking these devils, declare these scriptures over your life:

> "No weapon forged against you will prevail, and you will refute every tongue that accuses you. This is the heritage of the servants of the Lord, and this is their vindication from me," declares the Lord.
>
> —Isaiah 54:17, NIV

> I can do all this through him who gives me strength.
>
> —Philippians 4:13, NIV

> The Lord will make you the head, not the tail. If you pay attention to the commands of the Lord your God that I give you this day and carefully follow them, you will always be at the top, never at the bottom.
>
> —Deuteronomy 28:13, NIV

> Yet amid all these things we are more than conquerors and gain a surpassing victory through Him Who loved us.
>
> —Romans 8:37, AMPC

> I am the Lord, the God of all mankind. Is anything too hard for me?
>
> —Jeremiah 32:27, NIV

> He was pierced for our transgressions, he was crushed for our iniquities; the punishment that brought us peace was on him, and by his wounds we are healed.
>
> —Isaiah 53:5, NIV

> God anointed Jesus of Nazareth with the Holy Spirit and power, and how he went around doing good and healing all who were under the power of the devil, because God was with him.
>
> —Acts 10:38, NIV

Praise the LORD, my soul; all my inmost being, praise his holy name. Praise the LORD, my soul, and forget not all his benefits— who forgives all your sins and heals all your diseases.

—PSALM 103:1–3, NIV

Pastor David Wilkerson was my mentor and spiritual father. I remember when he would tell me, "John, God is married to His Word. You can hold Him to His promises and His Word. He will deliver 100 percent, all the time." Those words were grafted into my heart and spirit forever. Think of my late pastor's words as you pray the fire prayers. But before you begin, take a few minutes to worship and praise the Lord. Confess your sins. You don't want any hindrances to keep you from receiving God's best as you pray.

FIRE PRAYERS

I command every evil sickness and every infirmity spirit that has been planted in my body by the devil to loose my body now, in the name of Jesus. (Name each sickness. Lay your hands on your head or wherever the sickness is. Then, with the anointing and fire of the Holy Spirit, command that devil to come out, in the name of Jesus.)

By the fire of the Holy Spirit, I ask the Holy Spirit to purify and sanctify my body from all demonic pollution and every demonic sickness and infirmity that has gripped my body, in Jesus' name.

I ask the fire of God to roast and completely destroy, dismantle, and uproot every sickness. (Call out the name of any sicknesses and tell them to leave now, in the name of Jesus.)

I curse pain to its root. Let it shrivel up, die, and leave my body now, in Jesus' name.

I destroy every cancer devil and cancer cell. I command them to leave now, in the name of Jesus.

In Jesus' name, I destroy any issue of high blood pressure in my body.

I destroy diabetes and command it to leave my body, in the name of Jesus.

I release the arsenals of heaven against any oppression and depression that have overtaken my mind, heart, and thinking. I destroy all of it by the blood of Jesus. Release me now, in Jesus' name.

I bind the strongman of sickness over my bloodline on my father's side and on my mother's side. I curse it to the root. Let it shrivel up and die now, in the name of Jesus Christ.

I destroy every satanic or demonic altar and every sickness and infirmity that has been sent by witchcraft to destroy me. Let it be sent back to the senders and fall on their heads, in Jesus' name.

In the name of Jesus, I destroy all premature death in my family's bloodline, in my life, and in my descendants' lives.

I completely and fully destroy all pharmakeia, *including all demonic medications, pills, and treatments that have addicted my body. I curse them to the root. Let them shrivel up and die, and let my body be healed now, in Jesus' name.*

I destroy completely and fully all asthma, all bronchitis, and all COVID-19 devils and every respiratory issue that has blocked my lungs. I curse them now, in Jesus' name.

I release the anointing and fire of God through my family's bloodline, all the way down to Adam and Eve, to purify, sanctify, and make me whole and complete, in Jesus' name.

Father, in the name of Jesus Christ, I am healed, whole, and delivered out of the devil's hands and from every kind of infirmity spirit.

Lord, my Healer, I praise and worship You, and I give You all the glory. In Jesus' name, amen.

Chapter 31

PRAYERS TO DESTROY PREMATURE DEATH OVER YOUR FAMILY

AFTER TWENTY-FIVE YEARS as a hit man for the devil's kingdom, I was familiar with the devil and the spirit of premature death. I learned how to hurt and even destroy people's lives by bringing premature death into their families. The goal was to inflict pain and every kind of demonic consequence that is tied to this curse. I am grateful that all my guilt and shame for these acts are under the blood. So please don't go Pharisaic on me. I have faced my sins, and Jesus has set me free.

It is time to put any devil of premature death in its place. In the previous chapter we talked about illnesses that repeat themselves in bloodlines. All of them—cancer, diabetes, high blood pressure, heart attacks, mental anguish, and many other afflictions—can cause people to die before their time. I believe premature death devils bring these infirmities, and when no one curses them to the root, even young people can die too soon.

Premature death, whether from illness or suicide, is never God's will for us. It is a curse, straight from the pit of hell. We need to name the devils that carry the curse of premature death. Then we need to curse, renounce, and destroy them so we can live the abundant life God created for us (John 10:10). The fire prayers in this chapter are arsenal prayers that will bring down any targets in the devil's camp that have your name on them. Every sickness, every tormenting devil that brings suicide, and every devil of sickness or premature death will be destroyed, never to rise again. As you open your mouth and put God's fire on these devils, they will die and your loved ones will be released.

As you pray, remember that your precious days are in the hands of almighty God, who will not cut them short (Ps. 31:15; 139:16; 91:16). Hallelujah to His name!

171

FIRE PRAYERS

I call out every premature death devil that is taunting, plaguing, tormenting, and trying to cut short my family's bloodline through any form of premature death, including sickness, accident, and suicide. Come out now, in Jesus' name.

I release the fire of the Holy Spirit on all premature death demons' heads. Let the judgment of God fall on them and destroy them all. I release myself, my family, and my loved ones now, in Jesus' name.

In the name of Jesus, I come against every form of premature death that is trying to take my life.

Let the fire of the Lord Jesus Christ burn and completely purge from my family's bloodline all kinds of premature death, including those resulting from the words of my own mouth. Let these demonic plans be destroyed, in Jesus' name.

Premature death, I serve you an eviction notice now. In Jesus' name, drown now, in your own vomit.

Spirit of premature death, I curse you to the root. In the name of Jesus Christ, shrivel up and die.

Premature death that is trying to swallow up my life before my time, I smite your head seven times with the blood of Jesus.

I curse to the root every form of premature death that I have partnered with through words I have spoken over my life, family, or loved ones. In Jesus' name, amen.

By the blood of Jesus, I rip out of my family any premature death devils now, in Jesus' name.

In the name of Jesus, I suffocate every demonic premature death devil that is set against me. Come out and release me, in Jesus' name.

Oh God, let every premature death spirit die and permanently release me, my family, and my bloodline. Destroy every curse, vex, and sickness, as well as every repeating negative pattern and cycle and all voodoo. Let it all drown in the blood of Jesus.

By the fire of the Holy Spirit, I cancel every premature death devil against my life. In Jesus' name, amen.

In the untouchable and mighty name of Jesus Christ, I declare that I shall live and not die and declare the works of the Lord (Ps. 118:17). I will see His goodness in the land of the living (Ps. 27:13).

I disconnect myself and all my family members including my wife and child(ren) from any form of premature death. In Jesus' name, amen.

In the mighty name of Jesus Christ, I curse to the root all satanic forces that are trying to terminate my life prematurely.

Premature death, I give you your own death certificate now, in the name of Jesus.

By the fire of the Lord Jesus Christ, I declare that all the days of my life are already counted, blessed, ordained, sanctified, and covered by the blood of Jesus Christ (Ps. 139:16). My family and I declare and decree the goodness of God in the land of the living (Ps. 27:13). We will enter heaven when Jesus Christ calls us and not before. In His name I pray. Amen.

By the blood of Jesus Christ, I destroy every COVID-19 symptom that would try to bring premature death.

I destroy every COVID-19 devil, in Jesus' name. I command any premature death that would try to come through the disease or the vaccine to loose me now, in Jesus' name.

Let every demonic side effect that would try to bring premature death through any vaccine be destroyed, in Jesus' name.

I curse any premature death that would take any baby through abortion, killing the baby and the baby's purpose, which is to be part of the church of Jesus Christ. Let the premature death of abortion shrivel up and die, in Jesus' name. We curse to the root every abortion spirit, completely and fully, in Jesus' name.

Lord God, I give You glory, honor, and praise for who You are and for Your deliverance from every form of premature death.

Chapter 32

PRAYERS TO DESTROY DEMONS THAT HINDER YOUR BREAKTHROUGH AND BLOCK YOUR DESTINY

H AS THE THOUGHT ever popped into your mind that as a believer you should be further along in life and should already know your purpose and destiny? Do you feel some spiritual bungee cord snapping you five steps backward every time you take three steps forward?

I have been on the edge of a breakthrough when something way out of my control happened. One minute I was on the edge of my promised land, and the next minute I couldn't put two and two together. This happens to everyone at some point, but when it happens year after year and brings continual frustration, disappointment, and discouragement, it's time to get to the root issue. Otherwise, depression and oppression could be next.

There are people today, wonderful believers, who go on a first job interview and then a second interview. They are so close to their promised land of receiving an offer or acceptance from a firm or other organization. Then, out of nowhere, the doors close, and they get spiritually kicked back. Everything demonically falls apart. They get so close to the blessing, but that demonic bungee cord yanks them back. Everything that seems to be promising and looks like a victory becomes a spiritual disaster instead.

It's time to fight back.

Chronic blockages don't happen by accident. Wicked spirits are assigned to bring hindrance, delay, blockage, and distraction to undermine your identity and relationship with the Lord Jesus Christ. The devil wants to keep you in the dark about who you are and why you are here. He wants to block all revelation and clarity about your destiny and God's blueprint for your life. Even if you are already walking in God's purpose for your life, similar blockages can delay your next step.

The devil is a master of distortion and distraction. He erects supernatural, demonic roadblocks to test you and obscure God's character. He wants your relationship with God to grow cold. It's easy to worship and glorify King Jesus when you are in green pastures. But when demons stall your breakthrough, you can be tempted to see God differently. That is *exactly* what the devil wants.

It's time to destroy these stubborn spirits and completely dismantle the devil's agenda. Let's get violent and nasty with them and let them know that they can't keep you from what God has given you. By the power of the Holy Spirit, you will be victorious. You will be more than a conqueror in Jesus Christ (Rom. 8:37) because He is writing your story.

FIRE PRAYERS

By the blood of Jesus, I destroy every devil that is trying to invade my purpose and destiny.

I smite with the judgment of God the head of every demon of satanic hindrance, blockage, and delay. In Jesus' name.

In the name of Jesus, I set the fire of God to ambush every demon that is trying to slow me down or trip me up on the way to my promised land.

I release the fire of God on every demon that brings hindrance, delay, and blockage to my purpose, destiny, family, loved ones, ministry, and finances. Let them all be destroyed, completely and fully, in Jesus' name, amen.

I break the chains (the bungee cords) that are pulling me back to my past and stopping my movement toward the amazing things Jesus Christ has prepared for me.

Father, in Jesus' mighty name, let every satanic agent that is causing blockage and delay drown in the blood of Jesus now.

I speak to every demonic mountain and roadblock that is trying to prevent my steps to the finish line of my purpose and destiny. Let every scheme against my family, marriage, child(ren) (my inheritance), ministry, and relationship with the Lord Jesus Christ be completely and fully destroyed today.

In Jesus' name, let the fire of the Holy Spirit burn to ashes every demon that is blocking my breakthrough.

Let every devil that is hindering and blocking my promotion in my work and career drown today, in the blood of Jesus.

Father, let the favor of the Lord Jesus Christ open every door that the devil has closed in relation to my purpose, destiny, ministry, marriage, child(ren), family, church, and finances, in Jesus' name.

Father, let the oil of heaven be poured on my head as it was on Aaron's (Ps. 133:2), from the top of my head to the soles of my feet. I declare a fresh anointing on me, my marriage, my child(ren), and my family. Everything the devil meant for evil will be turned around for good (Gen. 50:20), in Jesus' name.

Father, let the anointing of the Holy Spirit be poured over every area of my life. Let every hindrance, delay, blockage, and distraction devil drown and be uprooted. Let every enemy assignment against my life be canceled, in Jesus' name.

Father, in Jesus' name, I declare that You will put Your finger on all known or unknown hindrances and delays in my life and destroy them now. In Jesus' name, amen.

Father, in the name of Jesus, I dip arrows in His precious blood and shoot them into the devil's camp. Let them destroy every demon that has been assigned to attack my purpose and destiny.

Father, in the name of Jesus, I destroy every demonic plot, scheme, and wile and every devil that has been assigned to destroy my purpose and my destiny.

In Jesus' name, I release the arsenals of heaven and the judgment of God on every foul and wicked spirit that is trying to intercept my purpose and destiny.

Father, I baptize myself and my family, loved ones, church, ministry, purpose, and destiny in the blood of Jesus Christ. Let every blockage, hindrance, and stronghold that is stopping my breakthrough be completely and fully pulverized. In Jesus' name, amen.

Lord, I give You the glory, praise, and honor. I worship You and thank You for Your victory, in Jesus' name.

Chapter 33
PRAYERS TO DESTROY
FINANCIAL HINDRANCE

EVERY MAN TO whom God has given riches and possessions, He has also given the power and ability to enjoy them and to receive [this as] his [allotted] portion and to rejoice in his labor—this is the gift of God [to him]" (Eccles. 5:19).

I understand that a perverted prosperity gospel is being promoted by preachers and others in the body of Christ today. It is centered on self-gain and self-gratification. It indulges the spirit of mammon and lust and has hurt the body of Christ greatly. At the same time, many Christians prefer a spirit-of-poverty perspective, thinking it makes us holy and acceptable to God. Neither view is right or true.

I believe God gives us opportunities to gain wealth for very good reasons: (1) so we can further the kingdom of Jesus Christ by helping ministries win souls, support missionaries, help people, and build and plant churches, and (2) so we can provide for our families, which includes keeping roofs over our heads and food on our tables, owning decent cars, paying for our kids' education, enjoying nice restaurant meals, and even taking annual vacations so we can rest and create memories together. I believe these blessings honor God.

DESTROY THE CANKERWORM AND THE LOCUST

The devil has other ideas. He is a master at dismantling finances and wants you to adopt or inherit a spirit of poverty. He knows the damage it can do. Many beautiful Christian marriages have been destroyed by financial lack. The devil releases his locusts (demons) to eat up your finances, hinder the Lord's blessings, and deceive you with trickery.

I'm not saying that we should worship money. We should be responsible stewards of everything God gives us. But it's time we dismantled the demons and forces that have hindered our finances and kept us from being entrepreneurs. Please realize that the devil sends curses on people's

179

finances. I have done that work in the witchcraft world; I have put curses on people's money so they would struggle and even lose their jobs and careers. It *happens.*

Even today, witches and warlocks sometimes attend my events and seek me out with their "love offerings." They want to personally hand me their money. So they get in my face and tell me, "I want to bless you with this. I want to give you this gift." They have the Christian lingo down pat, but they prepare that money for witchcraft. They want me to put it in my pocket and curse my own finances. Praise God for the Holy Spirit who enables me to discern their tricks. When I grab the money from a witch's hand, I give it to an usher or to someone else in the body of Christ and say, "Here, go to lunch on me." I can't keep the money because the curse is meant for me. But the curse is not meant for other people. They can take that money and use it.

The devil has many tricks. He can put a spirit of mammon on you to control and manipulate you. That spirit will keep you chasing wealth. But it's like chasing the wind. This chapter is not about chasing wealth. It's about resisting the spirit of mammon, stewarding what God gives you, and blessing the kingdom first. Like Matthew 6:33 says, "First and most importantly seek (aim at, strive after) His kingdom and His righteousness [His way of doing and being right—the attitude and character of God], and all these things will be given to you also."

Discern the Truth, and the Truth Will Set You Free

God's Word gives us amazing promises, like the one in Matthew 6:33. But it also gives us warnings about money. Let me share one promise and one warning before it's time to pray.

> I will give you the treasures of darkness [the hoarded treasures] and the hidden riches of secret places, so that you may know that it is I, the LORD, the God of Israel, who calls you (Cyrus the Great) by your name.
>
> —Isaiah 45:3

> No one can serve two masters; for either he will hate the one and love the other, or he will be devoted to the one and despise the

other. You cannot serve God and mammon [money, possessions, fame, status, or whatever is valued more than the Lord].

—MATTHEW 6:24

Both scriptures are for all believers. Personally, I do not believe that we in the body of Christ are called solely to nine-to-five jobs. I believe we are called to be entrepreneurs and to have careers in high places, where we are to represent the Lord Jesus Christ. But the devil has brought hindrances, delays, blockages, and distractions. I think we often define ourselves by our DNA, meaning we allow ourselves to be defined by which family we were born into. But God has given us a new DNA, and we can create wealth regardless of our family histories. It doesn't matter what our zip code is either. We are called to help ministries that faithfully advance the kingdom of Jesus Christ, win souls, baptize and disciple people, and equip them to do the Lord's work.

These are great works in the kingdom. But the devil's game plan is to stop us from being involved in them financially. We need to stop him instead. So let's pray.

FIRE PRAYERS

I curse to the root every demonic spirit released against me to dry up my finances. Let it shrivel up and die, in Jesus' name.

Spirit of mammon, the Lord rebukes you now, in Jesus' name.

I bind mammon and break all assignments of poverty against my life and my bloodline. In Jesus' name, amen.

I break the demonic powers of every satanic priest that has cursed my finances, and I wash my finances in the blood of Jesus Christ. In Jesus' name, amen.

In Jesus' name, I reject all satanic money that is sent my way to curse me and my finances.

I reject, renounce, and destroy every demonic lust spirit over me, over any uncertain finances, or over anything that seems to be a blessing but isn't. If the name of our Lord Jesus Christ isn't on it, I don't want it. It is only a setup and entrapment of the enemy.

Father, in Jesus' name, I loose any finances that the spirit of mammon is hindering.

O, Lord, open doors of financial opportunity over my life, in Jesus' name.

O, Lord, let every family curse that is trying to incarcerate my finances be uprooted now, in Jesus' name.

I curse to the root every devil that is tied to my finances, in Jesus' name.

Let the fire of God rain on every mammon devil that is hindering my finances today, in Jesus' name.

In the name of Jesus, I curse to the root all witchcraft that is done over my finances.

In Jesus' name, I curse to the root every satanic collection agency and every bankruptcy devil that Satan wants to send my way.

I disconnect my maternal and paternal bloodlines from every demonic financial curse, in Jesus' name.

I disconnect my family from every poverty spirit, in the name of Jesus Christ.

In Jesus' name, I break every demonic curse or manipulation that has caused me to spend money unnecessarily.

In Jesus' name, I destroy every plot, scheme, and wile of the enemy that is designed to cause financial failure in my life.

With the blood of Jesus Christ, I destroy the devourer over my finances.

I break the powers of every demon of deception over my finances. In Jesus' name, amen.

By the blood of Jesus, I loose my finances and all my potential to create wealth.

I cancel every demonic debt in my family's bloodline, in the name of Jesus.

Let the spirit of lack be burned down by the fire of the Holy Spirit, in Jesus' name.

Father, give me the wisdom and knowledge to create wealth for my family and advance the kingdom of Jesus Christ on the earth. In Jesus' name, amen.

Lord, open the windows of heaven and pour out a financial blessing that will overtake me and my family, in the name of Jesus.

Thank You, Lord, for purifying, cleansing, and redeeming my finances. Please give me the wisdom, knowledge, revelation, and clarity of spirit to balance my checking account, manage my income, and handle my financial accounts as a great steward who bears fruit in all seasons (Ps. 1:3). In Jesus' name.

Lord God, I worship You in spirit and in truth (John 4:24). Thank You for keeping me always. In Jesus' name, amen.

Chapter 34

PRAYERS FOR SELF-DELIVERANCE

TODAY, THE CHURCH at large lacks understanding, revelation, and clarity concerning deliverance and how people need to be delivered. Many ministers have declined to trust the Lord for their congregations, even though many precious brothers and sisters are under satanic and demonic attacks. But Jesus said that deliverance is the children's bread (Matt. 15:18–28).

Somehow, we believe that when we are saved, every wicked thing or any generational curses or satanic agreements that we had before we came to Christ automatically fall off us. Salvation does bring us into the kingdom, but healing and deliverance continue after that. Some things came off right away when I came to faith in Jesus Christ, but some satanic strongholds and bondages stuck around. The Holy Spirit had to walk me through the process so that, in God's timing, they came off and He set me free. That is what I call self-deliverance.

You need self-deliverance when any oppression, depression, or other satanic or demonic attack that hinders, delays, blocks, or distracts you keeps you from moving forward spiritually. These things incarcerate your mind so the enemy can manipulate your thoughts. You can have self-deliverance in your home or anywhere by utilizing your own faith and the power of the Holy Spirit. Your trust, faith, and deliverance come from Him and from your trust in the Lord Jesus Christ and His anointing.

As you pray the fire prayers in this chapter, something significant will happen: by the power of the Holy Spirit and in the name of Jesus, you will put on notice and evict every demon that has trespassed in your life, mind, heart, or body.

Please listen carefully: before you pray these prayers for self-deliverance, *you must do the following*:

- Make a list of things you need to know from the Holy Spirit about any strongholds, bondages, generational curses, or demonic experiences. As you proceed, let Him guide you through your confession of sins, repentance, renunciations, and forgiveness of others. List all devils, afflictions, self-inflicted wounds, and everything in your bloodline. List every demonic door, portal, and gateway that you might have opened. (As you pray the prayers, name these things and command them to release you, in the name of Jesus.)

- Confess your sins to the Lord.

- Have some paper towels and buckets ready. Demonic forces sometimes come out through burping, yawning, and even vomiting.

- Find a comfortable place where you will not be distracted.

Ready? Let's pray.

FIRE PRAYERS

Father, in the name of Jesus, I repent of all my sins. (Be specific.)

Lord, in Jesus' name, I thank You for who You are and for the love I know You have for me.

I call on warring angels from Michael's quarter to come down and remove every demon and take it to where the Lord wants it to go.

I dip myself, this room, and this whole place in the blood of Jesus.

Holy Spirit, I ask You to take over my deliverance, in Jesus' name.

I put on notice every demon that has been tormenting me: come out of me today, in Jesus' name.

In the name of Jesus, I break, destroy, and uproot any legal ground that I have given to any demon, whether known or unknown.

I break off me all generational curses of rebellion, witchcraft, lust, poverty, pride, idolatry, egotism, death, premature death, destruction, sickness, infirmity, and fear. I break off every mind-control devil. All rejection and self-rejection, come out of me now, in the name of Jesus.

I break off me every spirit of pharmakeia, drug addiction, and alcohol addiction. Come out of me now, in the name of Jesus.

I break and destroy every bloodline demon of infirmity in my father's and mother's bloodlines. Come out of me, in the name of Jesus.

I break and destroy the spirit of lust, fornication, adultery, masturbation, pornography, lust in my mind, lust in my eyes, fantasies, and lust fantasies in my mind and all spirits of perversion. Come out of me, in the name of Jesus.

All spirits of hurt, rejection, self-rejection, unworthiness, discouragement, depression, and unforgiveness, come out of me now, in Jesus' name.

187

I break off me all works of grief devils, all effects from every person who hurt me, every effect of having my heart broken, and all bitterness, anger, and sadness. Come out of me now, in the name of Jesus.

I command every spirit of manipulation, witchcraft, adultery, and fearmongering; every evil word that I or anyone else has spoken over my life; and every form of mental illness to come out of me, in the name of Jesus.

I speak to all unforgiveness, hurt, and pain caused by any betrayal devil or person who has let me down or used me for the wrong reasons. Come out of me now, in the name of Jesus.

I break the spirit of stubbornness, pride, anger, and bitterness; every root of disobedience, self, and self-will; and every ignorance devil that has incarcerated my mind and kept me from receiving what God has for me. Come out today, in the name of Jesus.

I command every sickness that has taken over my body, any lung issue (including asthma and COPD), every heart ailment and heart attack, all aspects of COVID-19, every symptom of monkeypox, all high blood pressure, and diabetes to come out of me now, in Jesus' name.

I curse to the root every issue relating to barrenness and the inability to reproduce. Come out of me now. I will have a baby, in Jesus' name.

Every spirit of cancer, come out of me now, in the name of Jesus.

Every demon of headache, migraine, head pressure, high blood pressure, colds, sinuses, bronchitis, flu, coughing, dizziness, and allergy, come out of me now, in the name of Jesus.

I break off me every spirit of doubt, fear, and unbelief, as well as every false prophecy, false teaching, and religious devil that has entered my spiritual space and atmosphere. Come out of me, in the name of Jesus.

In the name of Jesus, I command every generational curse in my mother's, father's grandmother's, and grandfather's bloodlines, all the way back to Adam and Eve, to come out now. (Name each curse that you can identify.)

Every spirit of fear, come out of me, in the name of Jesus. (Name each fear.)

Spirit of torment, come out of me now, in the name of Jesus.

I break completely and fully every molestation and rape spirit, every abortion devil, every spirit of bestiality or masturbation, every form of sexual abuse, and every satanic abuse of any kind. (Name them individually.) *Come out now, in the name of Jesus.*

I break off myself every spirit of shame and guilt and command it to come out of me now, in the name of Jesus.

Father, I declare that You will fill every void in my life and in my sisters' and brothers' lives with the Holy Spirit. I break all backlash, retaliation, and revenge. Lord, trample those spirits right now, in the name of Jesus. Let all retribution or reinforcement devils shrivel up and die.

I will declare my victory. I will declare my self-deliverance. I am whole and complete in Jesus Christ. Jesus, I give You the glory, honor, and praise, and I thank You for my self-deliverance today. The things You have ahead are greater than the things I am leaving behind. In Jesus' mighty name, amen.

Chapter 35

PRAYERS TO DESTROY THE SPIRIT OF JEZEBEL

I T IS TIME to disgrace the devil called Jezebel. This demon, this principality, still roams the earth. We see it from 1 and 2 Kings all the way to the Book of Revelation. It's true and also very sad that this spirit has manipulated, controlled, and destroyed many churches, from the leadership to the pews. It has caused church splits, and some churches have shut their doors altogether. Still, we refuse to recognize Jezebel's work, take authority over it, or fight back.

It is time, with the authority of the Holy Spirit, to take back the house of God and return our ministries, homes, and lives to His perfect will. We need to purify God's house from this demonic influence and whatever spiritual residue it has left behind, starting from the leadership down to the last person in the congregation.

First, we need to be clear about the Jezebel spirit. We often think it is all about manipulation and control. It is, but there is also the spirit of Delilah, which is a spirit of adultery, lust, and perversion mixed in. Jezebel walks in very particular ways and seeks to control, rule, and conquer. The following are clues to Jezebel's operation and manifestations in people. Jezebel's spirit

- brings fear (caused Elijah to run—1 Kings 19:1–3)

- attacks ministers (oppressed Elijah—1 Kings 19:9–10)

- attacks the anointing and those who are anointed (Elijah hid himself in a cave—1 Kings 19:9, 13)

- causes people to do their own will, not God's

- creates the appearance of repentance, then attacks

- needs to be praised, elevated; causes people to worship themselves and get others to praise them

- promotes a possessive love that destroys and controls

- creates the impression of loyalty until someone disagrees or brings correction (then rebels against that person)

- does all that is asked when it fits the spirit's overall plan

- plants seeds of discord that often lead to conflict or division in a church

- uses others to carry out evil plans, yet essentially works alone

- has an agenda, but it's never God's or other people's

- ignores the voices of God and other people

- is very religious ("I heard from God, and He spoke to me.")

- seeks positions of authority to control, discredit, and destroy

- commits to no one

- seeks affirmation and significance

- has illegitimate authority

- is a convincing liar

This is how Jezebel carries out her assignment and brings unthinkable destruction. It's time to ask God to give you discernment and open your spiritual eyes. Put on the armor to destroy this devil once and for all—including its attributes and assignments against what God has entrusted to you as a minister, pastor, evangelist, leader, teacher, family member, or spouse. It's time to get rid of Jezebel for good.

FIRE PRAYERS

I release the four winds of heaven to blow and destroy every plot, scheme, wile, and entrapment of Jezebel on my life, ministry, church, and marriage, in Jesus' name (Ezek. 37:9).

I loose chaos on Jezebel's plans and schemes against my church, in Jesus' name.

I release the hounds of heaven to chase this wicked spirit, eat up her flesh, and lick her blood, completely and fully, in Jesus' name (1 Kings 21:23; 2 Kings 9:10, 36).

I paralyze every demonic spirit that is operating in alignment with Jezebel and the spirit of Delilah. I destroy any spirit of witchcraft, lust, seduction, and intimidation that has been released on my church, ministry, and home, in Jesus' name.

I destroy the spirit of manipulation, control, and rebellion, in Jesus' name.

In Jesus' name, I release the spirit of Jehu against the kingdom of Jezebel, her demons, and her false prophets, and I put the judgment of Jehu on her head.

I strip Jezebel of all demonic authority, and I leave her naked and powerless, in Jesus' name.

I destroy every demonic assignment against my finances, business, ministry, and home and every demonic plot that Jezebel has against me, in the name of Jesus. Let them burn to the ground and never rise up again.

I destroy every seduction spirit of every kind and every Jezebel demon that has been released on my church. Let them be destroyed by the fire of God, in Jesus' name.

I destroy every demonic prophecy spoken by Jezebel over my purpose, destiny, ministry, church, and home, in Jesus' name.

In Jesus' name, I destroy the demonic foundation of Jezebel.

Whether it's in the leadership or congregation, I evict every Jezebel and Delilah spirit from my ministry, and I command it to leave now, in Jesus' name.

Let all of Jezebel's demonic assignments spoken over my church be destroyed by the fire of God, in Jesus' name.

Let every demonic plot, scheme, and wile of Jezebel rot, shrivel up, and die, in Jesus' name.

I release the fire of the Holy Spirit on my church to expose all hidden agendas of Jezebel in my congregation and leadership. Let them be exposed now, in Jesus' name.

Let Jezebel and her demonic false prophets be evicted from my church now, in Jesus' name.

I destroy every Jezebel spirit that she tries to birth with a demonic assignment against my church, my ministry, or my anointing. In Jesus' name, amen.

In the name of Jesus, I destroy the complacent spirit of Ahab that operates in my church and stagnates my church's growth.

Let the blood of Jesus purify my church, home, family, finances, purpose, and destiny, in Jesus' name.

Lord, strengthen my life, congregation, calling, purpose, and destiny, in Jesus' name.

I break every satanic assignment, plot, and scheme that Jezebel uses in my church. I command it to be uprooted now, in Jesus' name.

Lord, I command the fire of the Holy Spirit to purify the four corners of my church, inside and out. Holy Spirit, You are welcome in my home, in the house of God, and in my marriage, today and forevermore. In Jesus' name, amen.

Lord, I give You glory, honor, and praise for purifying and sanctifying Your church. Let Your perfect will be on Your church, and let Your church reach the world for Jesus Christ. In His name I pray. Amen.

Chapter 36

PRAYERS TO DESTROY WITCHCRAFT AGAINST YOUR CHURCH

G OD'S WARNINGS ABOUT witchcraft have always been clear: He tells us not to touch any of it. The Book of Deuteronomy provides some details:

> There shall not be found among you anyone who makes his son or daughter pass through the fire [as a sacrifice], one who uses divination and fortune-telling, one who practices witchcraft, or one who interprets omens, or a sorcerer, or one who casts a charm or spell, or a medium, or a spiritist, or a necromancer [who seeks the dead]. For everyone who does these things is utterly repulsive to the LORD; and because of these detestable practices the LORD your God is driving them out before you.
> —DEUTERONOMY 18:10–12

I want to share what I know from being in the witchcraft world. Before knowing Christ, I was a general in the kingdom of darkness, and some of my demonic assignments against the church included laying demonic hands on the doors of churches and cursing them; laying dead animals on church doorsteps so the church's anointing would die; and even urinating in front of a church's doors and cursing it. The devil gave me many assignments like that against the church of Jesus Christ.

There is unchecked witchcraft *within* the church today. The spirits of antichrist, divination, and mixture are functioning inside the church's walls. In Acts 20:29, Paul says, "I know that after I am gone, [false teachers like] ferocious wolves will come in among you, not sparing the flock." His warning is for us. It's time to rise up and annihilate the forces of darkness inside and outside the church. We need to clean house spiritually; restore holiness in the house of God; and evict Jezebel, Ahab, and every demon, whether it involves worldly witchcraft or Christian witchcraft.

Pray these fire prayers violently against the kingdom of darkness and every spirit masquerading as an angel of light that has crept into the church. It's time for holy anger; let's release the fire of the Lord to cleanse His house and disperse every satanic visitor from our pulpits, our pews, and even the church restrooms. Get ready, locked, and loaded with the fire of the Holy Spirit. Let the devil know he is messing with the wrong house.

FIRE PRAYERS

God, You are a consuming fire. Let the enemies inside my church become uncomfortable as I release the fire of the Holy Spirit on them now, in Jesus' name.

In the name of Jesus Christ, I release a Holy Spirit earthquake to shake the foundations of my church.

I break and destroy every pride-spirit devil that has crept into my church, whether in leadership or through visitors. I serve them all eviction notices now. Come out, in Jesus' name.

I release the fire of heaven on every known and unknown Christian witch and warlock that has come into my church. Let that fire fall on them and remove them now, in Jesus' name.

In Jesus' name, I frustrate every plot, scheme, and agenda of every witch that has designed spiritual blueprints against my church.

I break and curse to the root the silver cord of any witch's astral-projecting in my congregation, church, and ministry. Let it shrivel and die, in Jesus' name.

I release the fire of God on all witches that have infiltrated our services, and I release God's judgments on their heads so they will come to repentance, in Jesus' name.

Lord, let the blood of Jesus Christ purify every seat in my church, in Jesus' name.

Let the blood of Jesus vomit every witch and warlock out of my church, in Jesus' name.

I curse to the root any witchcraft involving articles and objects that witches and warlocks have stolen from my church. I break and destroy all of it now, in Jesus' name.

I loose my church from every demonic altar from the north, south, east, and west that has my name or my church's name on it, in Jesus' name.

Lord, let the fire of God fall on my church the way Elijah's fire fell on the altar. Let it consume the offering of our lives. In Jesus' name, amen.

I command every demonic spirit of mixture to come out of my church now, in Jesus' name.

Every New Age devil, release my church now, in Jesus' name.

Every demonic false theology, release my church now, in Jesus' name.

Every Jezebel devil, whether in leadership or the congregation, come out of my church, shrivel up, and die, in Jesus' name.

Every Ahab spirit that has crept into my church, I put the judgment of God on your head. Leave now, in Jesus' name.

With the blood of Jesus, I wash away all witchcraft identification, marks, animals, and sacrifices and any devils that lay hands on my church. I curse them to their roots. Let them shrivel up and die, in Jesus' name.

In Jesus' name, I destroy every witchcraft meeting that has taken place in my church.

Let the terror of the Holy Spirit fall on every witch, warlock, divination act, and witchcraft spell that is over my ministry, purpose, and destiny. Release me now, in Jesus' name.

Let the fire of God fall on the head of the serpent and chop it off, in Jesus' name.

Let any path of the wicked that is assigned against my church and its members be diverted and uprooted. In Jesus' name, amen.

I cover my church and its members in the blood of Jesus now, in Jesus' name.

I send confusion to the devil's camp and any demonic agenda or assignment against my church, in Jesus' name.

I remove and curse to the root every stubborn devil, every manipulation devil, and every witchcraft devil now, in Jesus' name.

As for me, my church, my home, and my family, we will serve Jesus Christ all the days of our lives (Josh. 24:15).

Let the goodness and mercies of God be poured over my house, family, church, purpose, ministry, and destiny. In the unmatchable name of Jesus Christ, amen.

Father, we give You glory, honor, and praise for our deliverance. Thank You, infinite Spirit, for sanctifying us and renewing our minds, hearts, spirits, and souls. We will not negotiate or compromise, and we will surrender all to have all You offer. In Jesus' mighty name, amen.

Conclusion
NEVER GIVE UP

I N OCTOBER 1999 I left my body and ended up in hell. The cross of Calvary and Lucifer showed up, and there was a showdown. The devil was no match for the cross of Jesus Christ. I came back into my body, and Jesus Christ became my Lord and Savior.

Growing up in silent pain, despair, and poverty on the cold, hard streets of the South Bronx was tough. But I had an incredible mama who was both Mommy and Daddy to me and my brothers. I remember the good days when she would reach into her pocketbook and pull out two dollars for me and each of my brothers. She would send us out to Yankee Stadium to sit in the bleacher seats, which were the worst seats ever. We were so high up that we could barely see the players. Yet it was glorious. While we were in the stadium, we felt like important people sitting in the best seats of all.

Sometimes my mom would give us two dollars each to see three movies in one day. But our greatest adventures in the neighborhood happened during summertime, when we opened a fire hydrant and bathed in its icy water in the middle of the street. Those were the good old days.

Other days were not good. My dad was a warlock. On weekends he beat my mother. Fear and torment lived in our apartment, where he practiced witchcraft rituals, ceremonies, and cleansings. He would send us to the witch store to buy the ingredients he needed to gain power, control, and demonic "success."

The only high point with my dad was when he took me and my brother to the car wash. We rode through the wash and watched the water and bubbles hit the windows. We thought we were having a great time in some amusement park. Afterward my dad would take us to White Castle and buy each of us two hamburgers, some fries, and a small soda. Then we would make a U-turn and head back home.

One Christmas my dad gave me the only gift he ever offered me: a miniature television. Before I opened the box, he said, "Stupid, here's your gift. Merry Christmas."

In that moment, it felt as if the gift disappeared from my hands. Instead of Christmas morning being the highlight of the year, it wrapped me in more guilt and shame. All I wanted was my father's approval. But being a good dad was hard for him. He never had one himself. There was no role model for him to learn from, so demons and principalities ruled and owned him. He was their puppet. He didn't realize they would be his demise.

My last memory of my dad is from a rainy October night when my aunt rushed into our apartment yelling and screaming that my father was dead. My mother jumped off the sofa and put on her coat. In the pouring rain we took the five-minute walk to the social club where my dad liked to hang out. Social clubs, many of them illegal, were traps where people got drunk, got into fights, and lost their lives. That's what happened to my father.

I've already told you about when we first saw his body. To be honest, I was not heartbroken. Instead of crying, I think I sighed in relief knowing that the monster would not be coming home or beating up my mother ever again. So the funeral came and went, and my mom, my brothers, and I carried on the best we could—day by day, week by week, month by month, and year by year.

By the grace of God a light always shone in our dark times. We always saw the break of dawn and made it through. Later I got married, and in 1989 we had a daughter. It hurts to say that in her life I became the person I hated the most—I became my father. Because of my demonic contracts, ceremonies, devotions, dedications, and satanic lifestyle, I missed out on being a good dad. I thank God that it's not where you start but where you finish that counts most.

IT'S NOT WHERE YOU START; IT'S HOW YOU FINISH

In October 1999 Jesus took the pen out of my hand and wrote my story. Despite the broken glass of the Bronx, my history with witchcraft and a devil-worshipping father, and the hundreds of buildings filled with lost souls, Jesus knew my address. That night when He visited me, I thought He made a mistake or picked me because I was the only one home. I now know that none of that was true. He makes no mistakes. I'm just glad that He found me. My life has never been the same.

A lot has happened since then. God took me out of the Bronx, placed me in Manhattan, and kept writing my story. One of the surprises He had in store for me was allowing me to meet the man who terrorized New

York City as a serial killer when I was thirteen. Claiming to be influenced by demons, he called himself the Son of Sam, and his murder spree kept the city on edge. Through it all my brothers and I went to school. We still smiled and laughed, watched baseball games on TV, watched our cartoons and sitcoms, and ate doughnuts or a pizza pie that my mother bought for dinner. We created our own fear-free fantasy world.

The Son of Sam was captured and eventually sentenced to 365 years in prison.[1] He is now a precious man of God and is called the Son of Hope. I have met with him in prison, prayed with him, laid hands on him, and studied the Bible with him. His life shows that God exists. It's a miracle, like my life is a miracle.

What matters is not my high school diploma or my natural DNA. It's not my broken childhood home, my misfit dad, the witches and warlocks, or the kingdom of darkness. It's not even the fact that I was a misfit dad as my dad was. What matters is that incredible encounter with Jesus Christ in 1999. That made all the difference to me.

God took my world and turned it into a universe. He redeemed my last name and gave me the anointing to write books and create e-courses. He has sent me to the remotest parts of the planet to preach the gospel. He sent me to First Nations American tribes in places most people don't know about. I have preached under tents, in the hard deserts of New Mexico, and in the upper reaches of Canada. I have been on seaplanes, propeller planes, jumbo jets, and boats that carried me from one remote island to another to bring the good news of Jesus Christ.

I tell you all this to say that there is hope for you. God writes amazing stories for His children. So please don't make permanent decisions based on your temporary circumstances. Give the pen back to Jesus, and you won't be disappointed. If you keep the pen, you'll spend your lifetime and your money buying correction fluid, and you will walk in circles. One of the scariest Bible stories is about how the Israelites started out in one place and went almost nowhere in forty years. They grew old, but they never grew up because they never wanted to leave the pen in the hands of a mighty God.

I thank the Lord Jesus Christ all the days of my life. I reflect on my past and on His goodness. His mercy endures forever, and He loves the misfit. If my story were in the Bible, it would be the one about the donkey that was tied up somewhere and Jesus said, "Go get him." He knew where the donkey was (the South Bronx), and He knew its condition (lonely and broken). Even though that donkey tried to start a life of his own, he accomplished nothing but only fell on his face—until the Master showed up and sat on his back. Then that donkey walked through Jerusalem (Broadway in New York City), proud to carry the Master and knowing that his life was moving from a place called Nowhere to a place called Somewhere.

That is the story of John Ramirez. Some people say my testimony is like the apostle Paul's, but I'd rather be that donkey with Jesus Christ on his back. That's my story. I am doing life in Jesus, and I want no parole. Until He calls me home, I'll gladly stay on death row.

Let that be your story, because Jesus Christ loves you. He is no respecter of persons, and He "shows no favoritism" (Rom. 2:11; Acts 10:34, NLT). Do what the psalmist did. He said, "I look up to the mountains—does my help come from there? My help comes from the LORD, who made heaven and earth!" (Ps. 121:1–2, NLT).

It's not where you start. It's where you finish. I had help from my heroes of the faith: Pastor David Wilkerson, Evangelist Nicky Cruz, and Evangelist Billy Graham. I thank God for Pastor David, who mentored me for three years in Times Square Church. Brother Nicky Cruz has touched my life in so many ways. What an honor! And Billy Graham—his sermons, his courageous attitude, and his uncompromised preaching prodded me to always preach the truth. As Pastor David Wilkerson told me, "Godly character and the fear of God will get you to the finish line, which is heaven."

I leave you with these last words: God is good. He knows your story, and He's writing your story. Make Him proud. Minister to His heart. He picked you, and you're no mistake. You are an orphan in the world's system, but Jesus walked into the world's foster care and adopted you. God is an incredible Father who knows all your needs. He knows your thoughts from afar. Lean on Him for all things. Acknowledge Him for everything. Be mindful of all He has done for you. Love Him like you have never loved anyone before. Honor and respect Him, and you will see signs, miracles, and wonders in your lifetime.

If I don't meet you in this life, I will meet you on Hallelujah Boulevard, and we will high-five, in Jesus' name.

Meanwhile, *never give up.*

NOTES

CHAPTER 3

1. *Merriam-Webster*, s.v. "edify," accessed November 11, 2022, https://www.merriam-webster.com/dictionary/edify.

CHAPTER 4

1. See Margaret Fishback Powers, "Footprints in the Sand," accessed November 11, 2022, https://footprintssandpoem.com/margaret-fishback-powers-version-of-footprints-in-the-sand/.
2. "Celebrating Jesus—The Light of Peace This Christmas," Kenneth Copeland Ministries Europe, accessed November 22, 2022, https://kcm.org.uk/celebrating-jesus-the-light-of-peace-this-christmas/.

CHAPTER 20

1. *Online Etymology Dictionary*, s.v. "incubus," accessed November 18, 2022, https://www.etymonline.com/word/incubus.

CHAPTER 21

1. Abigail Adams, "Homeless Man Charged With Murder for Allegedly Shoving Woman in Front of N.Y.C. Subway Train," *People*, January 16, 2022, https://people.com/crime/homeless-man-charged-with-murder-shoving-woman-in-front-of-new-york-subway-train/.

CHAPTER 26

1. Ed Stetzer, "Marriage, Divorce, and the Church: What Do the Stats Say, and Can Marriage Be Happy?," Church Leaders, January 20, 2017, https://churchleaders.com/pastors/pastor-articles/297689-marriage-divorce-church-stats-say-can-marriage-happy.html.

CONCLUSION

1. John Philip Jenkins, "David Berkowitz: American Serial Killer," *Britannica*, updated August 23, 2022, https://www.britannica.com/biography/David-Berkowitz.

Contact John Ramirez Ministries at

info@johnramirez.org.